I0026837

The Poisonous Garden

Anna Miller

Copyright © 2021 by Anna Miller
All rights reserved

First Edition

No part of this book may be reproduced, stored in a retrieval system, or
transmitted by any means, electronic, mechanical, photocopying,
recording or otherwise without written permission from the author.

Chapter One

2012

The damp soil stained my knees as they sank farther into the earth. My hands reluctantly dug around, searching for rocks to be pulled and removed from the garden plot. It was filthy work—nothing I wasn't used to, but that wasn't the point.

The situation was disgusting.

Humiliating.

God, and the dirt was everywhere. On my clothes, the tops and bottoms of my shoes, under my fingernails, between the lines of my palms, on my forehead when I wiped the sweat from my brow—*everywhere.*

Behind me, I felt him—no, *both* of them watching me as I worked. They didn't offer to help, they didn't comment, they didn't speak at all. They just watched me in silence as I picked stone after stone out of the ground and tossed them aside. Heat rose to my face from embarrassment, but I continued with my task, following the instructions given to me.

I'd been excited, at first, to be out here working on the plot. Loneliness and boredom can make someone desperate for activity, to get out of the house and *do* something with another person who wants you in their life. That's what I thought this garden would be for the two of us—a place for us to reconnect and bond and revive some semblance of love and a relationship. He brought me into this project, and I was overjoyed to be a part of something we could build together.

It wasn't in the cards, though. Not for him—not for his *plan*.

I wish I'd seen it. I wish I'd recognized why his interest in me suddenly rekindled, why he wanted me out there in the dirt and grime, toiling on my hands and knees as he watched. Longing will do that to you. It'll shroud your vision from everything that should set off your alarms. Blinders on the side, rose-colored glasses at the front. I saw what I wanted.

And any warning signs?

Well, I must have been *crazy* to imagine them.

Maybe if my head had been clearer, or if I'd taken a step back and let myself see the situation from fresh eyes, I would have realized what was happening. Fuck, maybe if I had talked to someone or gotten help—*real* help—I would have saved myself from all the heartache, paranoia, and fear. Maybe then I could have avoided the danger sooner.

Hindsight's a bitch like that.

I had no luxury of looking back, though, as I pried another coarse rock from the soil. My eyes stayed down and forward, the garden plot splayed before me, that toxic bed he made for me to lie in. Degrading as it was, I continued to work, ignoring the prying eyes and wondering why the hell I was doing this. And all by myself? With two other sets of able-bodied hands standing only a few feet away?

No. That wasn't the plan. Helping me would have been simple, and things were never simple with him. They were complex, meticulous, full of tricks and deceit. And oh, how I fell into it. I'd stepped into a world with promises of companionship and delight only to be ensnared in a trap where nothing but hazing and humiliation waited for me. Years of dependence held me to a life of power, control, and ritual—all culminating in that moment in the dirt. Meanwhile, he continued to loom behind my back, his mind was probably swirling and formulating and giddy with thoughts of his schemes and triumph as he spent the afternoon watching me.

Observing me.

Just like he'd done from the start.

1999

I came from a wealthy upbringing. My mother was a stay-at-home mom, but my father's occupation was fuzzy to me. He'd be out of the country for weeks on end to places like the Middle East and Venezuela. It was rare for him to talk about his job; he wanted a clear separation between work and his home life, and most of what I could gather was pretty vague—something about "government contracts." Whatever he did, it allowed us to live a luxurious life where everything was granted, and I wanted for nothing.

Growing up, I'd often go out with my friends and enjoy every flavor of fun the world had to offer us. It was a great life, full of excitement and very little worry, and I was totally content for things to stay as they were.

Of course, things changed after high school. My group of close-knit friends had scattered—everyone flittered off to attend different colleges out of state. Personally, I waited a few years before enrolling in Springfield State University to study sociology; it was close enough to home that I was able to continue living with my parents. Unfortunately, this meant I didn't experience the dorm life—where all the action was. Plus, I was twenty-five in a sea of eighteen-year-old freshmen, which made it harder to meet people and make connections at school.

Being the youngest in the family, my reaching adulthood had prompted my mother to enter the workforce as an event organizer for SSU. My father remained busy, continuing to make his business trips overseas. This left me alone for much of my time, and I felt isolated from the social crowd.

So when Katie, a girl I knew from class, invited me to a party one weekend, I couldn't turn down the opportunity to reclaim that feeling of connection I'd lost.

While SSU was a large school, it was nestled in a fairly small city. Everyone knew everyone in Greenville, and whenever someone planned a party, word spread like wildfire. The house was wall-to-wall bodies with loud music and a plastic cup of booze in every hand.

Exactly my kind of scene.

It was May 1st (a date now forever ingrained in my mind), and the late spring air was filled with ecstasy, freedom, and the smell of weed. As I engaged in the camaraderie and danced about and partook in a couple drinks, I began to feel like my old self again. I met people from all over town, not just other students from the college. It was a whirlwind of new faces and names I'd soon forget, and I lived for every savory second of it.

One guy in particular caught my interest, and I spent some time chatting with him—flirting with him too, because why not? He was sweet and charming and held my attention, so I let him give me all the attention I craved.

That was when I noticed... well, *him*.

He was positioned on the sofa across the room. Even through the crowd of sweaty, drunk bodies, I had a clear view of him. He was handsome with dark hair and dark clothes to match. His dark eyes were on me, burning, intense; I concluded he'd been watching me for a while. I gave him a fleeting look before returning to my conversation, but every time I glanced back over, his gaze was still fixed on me.

Eventually, he must have figured he'd spent enough time sizing me up and decided to make his move. He stood, and with a few smooth strides, he crossed the room and planted himself in front of me, damn near sweeping the guy I'd been flirting with aside to take his place. We locked eyes, and there was something in his face that held me there. I couldn't explain what, exactly, but a peculiar feeling swept over me. Like I'd been asleep this whole time, then abruptly awakened and brought to life by his sudden presence.

Wordlessly, he reached for the empty cup in my hand. My fingers released their grip like it was the most natural thing, and I let him take it. He passed the cup off to other guy, not peeling his eyes off me for a second.

"You should get the lady a refill," he said. It sounded like an order.

The guy I'd been flirting with stood straighter and spat out an, "Excuse me?" He sounded pretty indignant, insulted by the interruption, but his protests were met with silence and the side of my face as I favored the newcomer. The poor sap was already forgotten, and to this day, I couldn't tell you his name. Recognizing the newcomer and me were clearly enamored with each other, he decided to cut his losses and leave us be.

Once he was gone, the rest of the party faded with him. Katie, wherever she ended up, was miles away, and the music sounded muted, like it was playing in another room. This new man eclipsed everything around me until my vision was filled with nothing but his striking face. I inhaled, soaking up the moment of this meeting. I longed for him to say something, but he remained stoic and poised, waiting—daring?—for me to break the silence.

"Hey," I said, tucking a strand of long hair behind my ear.

"Hey." His voice was smoky, his smile devilishly handsome. "Your name?"

"Ruby."

"Ruby," he repeated. My name sounded brand new as it trickled from his lips, yet it seemed he was always meant to say it. Then his hand was wrapped around mine—I wasn't sure if he'd just grabbed it or if it had always been there. "Come with me."

My knowing, mischievous smile was all the confirmation he needed. He led me away, pulling me through the crowd and the winding turns of the house. His stride was confident and assured, like he knew the layout of the place perfectly. All the while, I grew increasingly enchanted by how bold the gesture was. It was like something from a movie, a fated encounter between star-crossed lovers. Our pace increased, soaring with my spirits as I eagerly followed him to wherever he was taking me.

When we found ourselves in a private room, our eyes met again. The second the door clicked shut, he ushered me to the bed and sat down next to me.

We stayed there for hours, smoking weed and launching ourselves into one of the deepest, most personal discussions I'd ever been a part of. I found it so easy to open up to him, indulging him in what felt like my entire life story. Somehow, I felt comfortable enough to even tell him about my prescriptions.

"Oh, you take Xanax?" he asked, raising an eyebrow.

"Only once in a while," I clarified. "Sometimes I get stressed or anxious, and it helps."

"I've heard college will do that to you," he said with a nod. "You should probably get more; never know when you'll need it."

I shrugged. "Maybe I should."

The conversation shifted to him and how he lived his day-to-day. I learned he was a cook, a profession he had a deep passion for.

"You know, most people assume cooks are just low-level workers. Not true," he said with an authoritative air. The smirk splayed across his face was intoxicating. "In fact, chefs, cooks—they're the most powerful people in the world."

"How so?" I asked playfully.

"Well, think about it." He leaned back, propping his elbow on a decorative pillow. "Everyone needs to eat, right? And what we eat shapes our bodies; it influences how we're built on a molecular level. Chefs control what people eat. Ergo, they must be the most powerful." He took a drag from the near-roached joint and blew smoke over my head.

My face stretched in a smile as I shifted my weight to the side and cocked my head, allowing my long hair to tumble down past my shoulder. "That's quite a claim," I teased.

He let out a breathy chuckle, suddenly bashful. "Sorry," he said. "Sometimes I get carried away. You're just so... You're so easy to talk to."

"I understand," I told him, soaking in that dashing, mesmeric grin of his. "It's like I've known you my whole life."

His hand grazed my cheek. "I feel the same."

Our faces were close, and our stares intense. Hungry. He wanted something. So did I. I wasn't drunk—I never was one for letting loose like that—but all the same, I let the influence of the night take over, and in an instant, my lips were on his and my back met the bed. Words lost meaning but held more weight than they ever had before.

How long we were there—talking, kissing, keeping busy—I couldn't say. Hands flew about, our clothes along with them. The world and its inhabitants melted away until there was nothing left but that secluded room and the hot air between us. It wasn't until we were lost and far into becoming intimately familiar with each other that I learned his name was Donovan.

I never did get that fresh drink.

Chapter Two

About a week went by.

Things quickly fell back into their normal routine of school, homework, and being alone; my sweeping night of romance was already beginning to fade into the background. Donovan and I had been too caught up in the moment to exchange information, and with no way to get back in touch, I feared I'd never get a chance to speak with him again.

Then, miraculously, I got a call from him. He told me, much to my elation, he'd been asking around about me and searching for a way to see me again. He'd finally hunted down my number from an acquaintance at school and hit me up. The sound of his voice reawakened the excitement I'd felt at the party, though it was different now. A phone call wasn't a one-off night in a college co-op. A phone call was something more.

I learned Donovan wasn't originally from the area and had been visiting some friends the other week. He lived about three-and-a-half hours away, but the distance wasn't enough to dash my hopes. As I listened to him speak, pleasing my ears with sweet, honey filled words, I waited for him to ask the right question.

At last, he requested I visit him. I agreed without a second thought.

Since the party, I had gone to the salon to have my long hair chopped into a cute pixie cut, as I'd been in the mood for a change of style. On the day I made the long drive to see Donovan, I wore an Avada necklace my sister had gifted me. It was one of those pendants you could infuse with a scent. Mine smelled like lavender, and I found it very soothing to wear. Plus, I wanted to look nice for the reunion, and the accessory brought my whole look together nicely.

The moment I showed up on Donovan's doorstep, he immediately took great interest in those details. He disappeared into his apartment and fished out a copy of the film *Rosemary's Baby.* A strange excitement filled him as he pointed out the physical similarities between me and the titular character, including her short haircut and an herb-filled necklace she wore throughout the film. He claimed it was his favorite movie and went into a giddy ramble about it. I found his enthusiasm cute.

We settled ourselves in his small living room, and even though the place was dirty and cramped, I was happy to be with him. We cuddled on his couch and talked some more, enjoying light caresses and the zen of the music from his stereo. He lit a couple joints for us to smoke, adding to the overall relaxed atmosphere of the afternoon. After a while, Donovan circled back to *Rosemary's Baby* and snatched up the DVD.

"We should watch it," he said. "It's *uncanny* how much you remind me of Rosmeary. I want you to see what I mean."

I giggled, taking a drag off my joint. "Alright, pop it in."

He did so with glee, then grabbed us a couple bottles of beer from the kitchen. Settling himself back on the couch, he opened his arm to me as an invitation, which I took gladly. I snuggled up against his side, feeling cozy as the film started playing.

It was… okay.

The pacing was slow for me, and the runtime was so long I grew a little bored early on. There were one too many scenes of people standing around in an apartment and gossiping about whatever-the-fuck. The surrealism of the satanic sex scene montage was confusing, and even when things started to get intense near the end with the birth of a demon baby, I struggled to understand the movie's appeal. One thing stuck out, though—Donovan was right. The haircut Rosemary got halfway through the film was nearly identical to mine, and she did indeed have a necklace infused with something herbal.

The similarities stopped there, however.

As the credits rolled, Donovan turned to me, face lit up like a schoolboy's. "What did you think?" he asked in earnest.

I bit my lower lip, wondering how I could express my opinion without offending him. A sip of my (second) beer bought me an extra moment to think. "Um... It was fine. A little slow, but... Well, it was crazy."

"Wasn't it?" he exclaimed, either not recognizing my hesitation or ignoring it. "I love the thematic elements—all the symbolism and metaphors. The writing's *so* smart!" He shifted on the couch so he was facing me. Puffing smoke out of the corner of his mouth, he said, "Ruby, the night we met was really special. You know why?"

I shook my head.

"It was May 1st, the day of Walpurgis Night."

"Gesundheit."

"*Walpurgis Night,*" he repeated with a smirk. "It's a European holiday where people celebrate warding off witches, but back in the day, it was said Walpurgis Night was when witches would meet on the highest peak of the Harz Mountains." He lifted his hand to demonstrate, and my eyes followed instinctively. I didn't bother to ask where the mountains were. "That date is a big deal, and it's the night we met."

I leaned forward, drinking in the way he was looking at me, the way his eyes seemed to shine as he spoke. Excitement and revelation pooled together in his expression. It made my chest swell.

"I think it was fate, Ruby," he said earnestly. "It's meant to be."

* * *

We started seeing each other regularly after that. Between my studies and his job, our visits were limited to the weekends. At the start, I'd often go to visit him, but the drive soon became too much for me, so we began holing up in cheap motels to spend the night getting high and fucking. I looked forward to our time together. Through my efforts to keep my grades up and my perpetual lack of a social life, my day-to-day life felt trivial and isolating. I was more alone than ever, and I craved those moments of doting and companionship. In those dingy hotel rooms, we created a special space for the two of us to exist outside the dismal world around us. Donovan became more than just a guy I was dating; he was an escape.

Along the way, he introduced a new substance into our escapades. On top of the weed and alcohol (the former of which I was becoming more and more familiar with) he brought some ecstasy with him—a small baggie of colorful tablets. I'd never tried it before and was nervous the first time he offered it to me, but he looked me in the eye and said, with immense assurance, "It's okay. I'll be here to take care of you."

How could I say no to something so sincere?

He offered me a round blue pill. I moved to grab it, but he pulled back, taking it out of my reach with a playful grin on his face. I got the message. Leaning forward with my mouth open, I let him place the pill carefully and seductively on my tongue. Thirty minutes of sobriety went by. Then something flipped the switch.

And holy shit, what a trip.

I felt free as a bird and happy as a fucking lark. It wasn't like weed, which mellowed me out and lulled me into a relaxing zen. No, this shit energized me to *high heaven*. A tsunami of invigoration hit me with a vengeance, and I felt I could jump off the bed and fly around the motel room like I was in fucking heaven! My heart rate soared with newfound confidence, and my hands could not keep themselves off Donovan. He laughed, amused by my first hard trip, and enabled the episode with kisses on my neck, thighs—wherever he could press to please me.

The rest of the night was a whirlwind of beer, weed, sex, cuddles, more beer, more sex, and so much more cuddling. It was like our first time together at the party but cranked up to eleven. Between bouts of erotic adventures, I lay on his chest and listen to both his heartbeat and everything he had to say. He told me about cooking, literature, and philosophy. Every word out of his mouth sounded amazing and full of wisdom. He was so smart, so well-read. I felt so lucky to be with such an individual.

In our state of happiness, the world outside again faded away. Gone from my mind were all thoughts of school, responsibility, and loneliness. The room was our realm, our oasis, our bliss.

Then it crashed like a bad accident. The ecstasy lost its magic, and my mood plummeted into a near depressive state, my energy utterly depleted. Still, Donovan was there. He cradled me and whispered sweet nothings and let me know everything was going to be okay. I believed him. I nestled into him and felt comforted by his embrace as he petted my head and hummed me to sleep.

For weeks and weeks, that's how it played out—days of being alone interrupted by weekends of love and escapism. Our visits fell into an almost ritualistic routine. We found a motel, we locked ourselves away, he put on some music and placed a pill on my tongue, and off we rode on the highway to hell. I didn't tell anyone the details of our meetups. Fear of judgment from family and peers aside, I wanted desperately for those days to remain ours and ours alone, for no intrusion or disturbance to interfere with our fun. During those nights filled with hot breath and cold air, I was free and he was sublime.

We were together, and all was right in the world.

Chapter Three

While Donovan was a fountain of knowledge and excitement, he was admittedly pretty hard up for cash. His cooking job at the restaurant only earned him ten bucks an hour—not exactly the most inspiring income for me, especially given my background. He brought up his money troubles now and again, and I decided no boyfriend of mine—now that we'd made it official—was going to struggle like that.

My parents had entrusted me with their credit card, and on top of buying whatever my heart desired for myself, I started putting it toward purchases for Donovan. I paid for his clothes, groceries, pretty much all of his expenditures but his rent. It felt good to take care of him like that. He'd been so good to me, after all. I craved his attention and didn't want to lose it.

Of course, I didn't let on to my parents what I was doing. I had a feeling they wouldn't approve. My mother, brother, and sister were already expressing ill will against Donovan. They didn't like his attitude, calling him arrogant and selfish. Their behavior was frustrating. They didn't know him the way I did. They had no idea how amazing he made me feel whenever he whisked me off to our enchanted nights of romance and revelry. I never tired of the thrill he gave me during our time away in those hotel rooms. He continued to be my escape from the dull life I lived outside of him. He was intelligent and attractive, and if they couldn't see it, that was their problem.

Weeks turned into months, the months into years, and Donovan and I stayed together. And while we lost ourselves in each other and the booze and the drugs, the world around us turned and filled itself with exciting events and tragedies. We saw the turn of the millennia, George W. Bush was elected, the US was shaken by 9/11, and shortly after, another horrible event occurred, this one closer to home.

It was all over the news—an international student from my old school, Cindy Song, went missing Halloween night after partying with friends. She was last seen after she was dropped off at her apartment in one of the student housing complexes in the early hours of the morning. Her friends found her apartment locked and undisturbed, though the bag she'd had with her the night before was there. But no Cindy.

She'd vanished.

And she'd lived not very far from me.

"You see?" said my mother in that maternal I-love-you-but-I-told-you-so way. "People are crazy. That might have been you if you'd moved into the dorms."

I shrugged, trying to play off the shudder crawling up my spine. "Yeah, maybe, but you know I'm careful," I replied.

"Yes, but I'm glad you're home where I know you're safe."

I told her not to worry, reminding her I didn't go out much anyway. If I wasn't home, I was either at school or with Donovan. As much as I enjoyed social interaction, I tended to keep to myself and my inner circle, and right now that circle was only big enough for two.

Donovan seemed pretty determined to stretch out that perimeter, though. He started taking me to visit his parents more frequently. They were nice enough people, albeit very, *very* religious. The family was devoutly Catholic, and their home was adorned with crucifix after crucifix with the occasional framed Bible quote or Jesus portrait to mix it up. I wasn't super religious, personally, and I felt a little uncomfortable when Donovan's mother asked which church I attended (none of them, to her disappointment).

Getting a glimpse into the atmosphere Donovan grew up in was telling, truthfully. I supposed spending his younger years in such a household was what sparked his interest in demons and the occult. It must have been the natural progression for those rebellious Catholics who decided church was too stifling. I imagined the one-eighty flip was a middle finger to the institution.

Dinner with Donovan's family was almost always awkward and stilted. Those monotonous hours of polite, cordial conversation made me feel like I was walking on eggshells, and one wrong step would make a crack loud enough to wake the dead. My concern about accidentally offending my hosts wasn't slaked when Donovan would afterward read too much into my clothes and actions, like I'd dressed or spoke a certain way on purpose to make some sort of grand declaration.

"I can't *believe* you wore red nail polish to their house," he said one day after an especially painful visit. He was amused, I could tell, but also halfway shocked on behalf of his parents. "Quite the statement to make, Ruby."

I didn't get it. "It... wasn't? I just like the color red."

"So do I," he responded with a smile. "Yet another reason we're so perfect for each other."

That handsome bastard made it so difficult for me to stay mad at him.

* * *

A few years into our relationship, Donovan moved to Greenville to be closer to me. I appreciated the gesture, as it meant I wouldn't have to be so far away from my family and home to be with him. Though... something changed in me after his move. The sudden closeness seemed to diminish the magic of our visits. Without the long travel time, meeting up with him didn't really feel like I was "escaping" anything anymore. Our nights of ecstasy and love had been pulled too close to home, and I found myself wanting to see Donovan less and less.

Then, one day, he decided to drop a bomb on me.

We were curled up in bed, hyped up on afterglow. He brushed away the hair from my face and stared deeply into my eyes. While I'd been adverse to him at the time, I couldn't deny that look of his still turned me to putty.

He took a deep breath, like he was about to say something important.

"Hey, Ruby…" It started so simply. "What are you doing next Thursday?"

I blinked, confused at the serious, sultry tone he'd assigned to such a basic question. "Nothing. Why?"

Shifting, he inched closer. "Do you want to get married?"

I shot up. "What?"

"Yeah!" He sat up to meet me. "Ruby, we're meant to be together, I can feel it." His hand was in mine. It was warm and welcome. "I mean, think of all the great times we've had. We should do this. We don't even need a big wedding or anything fancy; we'll just elope. You and me. We can even do it in secret if it makes you feel better. Everyone else will find out whenever we feel like telling them."

Needless to say, I was speechless. My heart soared at the gesture. Unorthodox as the proposal was, the thought of an elopement sounded like the most romantic thing in the world. It didn't help when he brought my hand to his lips and gently pressed them against my fingers.

"I love you, Ruby," he said wistfully. "Marry me."

God, he was just…

The logical side of my mind kicked into high gear, and I shook myself from my starry-eyed trance. "Okay, hold up!" I pulled my hand away, and the disappointment on his face was palpable. "L-look, you don't even have a real job. How are you supposed to take care of us, huh?"

He furrowed his brow, clearly thinking.

My mind sparked the idea first. "Donovan, I can't marry you unless you go to college and make something of yourself, something that will support us in the long run."

His eyes lit up with hope. "So if I enroll somewhere, you'll elope with me?"

My breath caught in my throat—*fuck*.

"Yes," I told him. "Yes, I will."

* * *

True to his word, Donovan enrolled in SSU to major in mechanical engineering—an impressive route for him to choose, I had to admit. He was smart, though, and I had no doubt he'd really make something of himself with a degree in such a prestigious field.

I thought about his proposal again, taking into account how eagerly he bent over backward to meet my criteria and please me. It was such a sweeping gesture, I found myself considering the idea just because of the leaps and bounds he was taking. The guy had committed to a four-year degree for my hand in marriage, for fuck's sake. How could I say no to that? Besides, the thought of an elopement was admittedly very romantic. The final, perfect chapter in our unorthodox courtship.

Maybe Donovan's point about fate would ring true.

So I agreed. I eloped with the man. It was May 1st, 2003, the four-year anniversary of our meeting. Walpurgis Night.

Donovan had it all planned out—the marriage license, what we'd have for dinner, the suite at the hotel. He even rented a limo to drive us around town to celebrate. The thought of it all thrilled me. It truly felt like a movie or some sappy special on television.

Of course, we told no one. It was agreed that everyone else—our friends, our family—would find out in due time and would simply have to accept our decision. We got everything settled at the courthouse in the span of an afternoon, then fled to the coziest room of the nearest hotel. The whole ordeal was filled with promises of devotion and giddy declarations of how happy we would be, how charming our future would become now that we were husband and wife.

All the while, my heart soared as I let myself get caught up in the excitement. Donovan even opened the limo door for me like a perfect gentleman and helped me step out of it. That night didn't see sleep until the small hours of the morning, as we were too occupied with drugs, booze, and (most importantly) each other. We lit candles and drank champagne and laughed deep into the night. I'd go so far as to call the evening *magical.*

Though, after I'd had a chance to sleep on things, I woke up the next morning feeling… Well, reality came crashing down on me as I realized the full extent of what just happened, and intrusive thoughts of regret swirled through my mind. You hear of people getting cold feet the day of their wedding; well, I got cold feet the day *after.* It hit me I could never go back, and the thought was startling, unnerving.

Laying in bed, contemplating my sudden circumstance, I entertained thoughts of annulment. It wasn't too late, was it? I could contact my parents and ask for the advice on what to do, how to reverse this, and they could help me, but… Fuck, what would they even *say*? Their youngest daughter had just married a guy they disapproved of without a single word of notice. I couldn't imagine they'd be so quick to offer their aid; they'd be far too disappointed in me. My face flushed with shame.

I sat there suffering in my emotional cocktail of regret and fear and anxiousness, unsure of what to do. But as Donovan came from behind me and kissed my neck, I thought, all right—I could do this. He cared for me, clearly, and we'd gone through all this trouble to be together; I might as well give this a fair shot. With Donovan taking care of me, we could be happy, us two. We'd grow old, keep each other company, and live a full life in each other's arms. Yes, I decided, this was a decision I could live with.

So I let fate take the wheel.

Chapter Four

Since my marriage to Donovan was kept secret, I had to carry on with life as though nothing had changed. I continued to live with my parents, pushing away the guilt of keeping this great, clandestine event from them. By then, I'd graduated from SSU, so I didn't have schoolwork to keep my mind occupied anymore. My mother and father remained busy as ever, and with Donovan working and attending university, his schedule became overloaded. I spent most of my time alone with my thoughts and decisions, wondering if I was doing the right thing.

While I tried to hold on to the hope things would work themselves out for the better, life started lobbing things at me that challenged my resolved. For starters, Donovan decided to change his major to English, a move that confused the hell out of me.

"What do you expect to do for a living with *that?*" I demanded.

He shrugged. "Reading and literature are things I'm passionate about, you know that. I figure until I find something, you could get a job and support us."

"What!?" I exclaimed, nearly laughing in his face. "Don, I am not the working type. *You* were supposed to become an engineer and take care of us. That was the deal." *That's why I fucking married him.*

"We'll figure it out," he said, devil-may-care. "Don't worry."

But I did worry. What the hell could he even do with a BA in English? B.S. was more like it. I didn't have very long to grumble about it, though, as my parents had figured out we were married. It wasn't something I could keep from them for very long, and I could tell by the way they confronted me about it they were disappointed. On top of that, they'd discovered I'd been using their money to support Donovan financially. My mother told me *he* needed to be the one supporting *me,* and she and my father decided to restrict my spending. I was still free to buy things for myself, but from then on, I was forbidden from using their money on my husband.

Donovan wasn't too happy about this revelation. He'd grown accustomed to the lifestyle he'd been living on my parents' dime and struggled to let it go. Though now the cat was out of the bag and word of our elopement spread around town, he came to visit me more often. Much more often, in fact, to the point where he nearly moved into my parents' house. He even started keeping his clothes there and spending almost every night with me. His dingy apartment had all but been abandoned, becoming our designated spot to get away for those times when we wanted to be alone.

It was admittedly an odd arrangement. A newlywed couple living under the bride's parents' roof when the groom had a place of his own wasn't the most traditional way of going about things, but then again, nothing about our relationship was traditional. Donovan did suggest I move in with him, but I simply said, "Hell no, I'm not living in that dirty place of yours," and that was that.

Some changes came over me. While I missed the thrill of those first years with Donovan, I found I wasn't as interested in the hard drugs anymore. I stopped taking them. Even when my husband and I took a day to be alone and partake in such substances, I turned them down. This offended him, for some reason.

"What, you think you're too good for this stuff now?" he asked.

"No," I said, a mixture of defensiveness and unease in my voice. "I just don't want to do them anymore."

"Whatever."

He asked me about my prescriptions again. I knew he'd been taking some of my Xanax pills here and there, and I was fine sharing those with him. This time, he suggested I get more of my Vicodin and Soma in addition to the Xanax. You'd think I would've told him no, absolutely not, but I felt I couldn't deny him. When I saw my doctor next, I asked for more pills.

And I got them.

Even though he was in school, Donovan continued to work. He bounced around different restaurants (finding a new, different problem with each of them) until he landed a position as a cook at a place called the Roadhouse Bar and Grill.

I was familiar with the place. Like I said before, everyone knew everyone in Greenville, and if there was underground information to be passed along, it always made its rounds through the Roadhouse. Everyone who attended the bar was a regular in some capacity, whether it be for the bar's services or the services occurring under the table. The nightly flirtatious transactions kept the local motels floating high above water, if you catch my drift.

It goes without saying, I hardly ever went. There was nothing in that bar I wanted to be a part of, and on the rare occasions I *did* go, I ended up leaving feeling regretful of encountering the people I'd met. Everyone understood what the Roadhouse was all about. It was a hub of the worst kept secrets, and I was sure there was some corrupt reason the police never shut it down. Because of this, the biggest players in the Roadhouse became apparent to me. One of them was a man I would never forget: a cook named Tomas.

Tomas was from Central America—Panama, if I remembered right. He was one of those guys everyone seemed to know. I'd hear people talk about him now and again, and from context clues, I learned his story. He'd started as a low-level drug dealer and had (allegedly) climbed his way up the ladder until he was the head of several drug rings. I assumed the Roadhouse was his main office of operations, but of course, I asked no one about it.

I didn't have many interactions with Tomas. I mostly observed him from afar while trying to remain invisible to the other patrons by staying in my seat. One night, he was out on the floor chatting with some people when he made his way over to Donovan and me. They spoke a little, mostly talking about work, but the conversation somehow weirdly drifted to Cindy Song, whose disappearance had become a cold case.

"Oh, yeah," said Tomas, lowering his voice like he was sharing something dark and secret. He leaned closer to us. "Bet you wouldn't guess, but I know what happened to her. She's dead now, but I know exactly where she was kept." His tone was boastful, proud. It didn't come off to me as a tall tale used to impress people.

It worried me when he and Donovan became good pals.

* * *

After a time, it grew apparent we needed to get our own place. Having Donovan and my parents in the same living space was just too awkward, and if we were going to be a married couple, we needed a proper household to start a life in.

House hunting was a headache. Given my unemployment and Donovan's meager wage as a cook, there weren't a lot of options available to us. The ones that were within our range were gross, cramped, and not in the best neighborhoods. We bickered over what to do about our situation. I again brought up that if he'd stayed on the engineering track, we wouldn't have this problem. He dismissed the comment.

In the greatest bout of good luck on the planet, a good house ended up falling into our laps. My friend Julia heard of our struggles and told me about her parents' townhouse. They were keeping it as a second home for vacations but were figuring out the upkeep of two different houses was too much to handle for them in their old age. I'd known Julia's family for years, and her parents regarded me as a second daughter. They kindly offered their house to us, lowering the price well within our range. They'd even keep all the furniture, décor, and kitchenware in there, meaning Donovan and I would want for nothing.

It couldn't have been more perfect. Everything was set; all we needed to do was move in with our stuff. And even though I was leaving the nest, my mother told me they'd still support me financially. I began to grow hopeful. Maybe now with Donovan and I owning a place of our own, things would spark back to life. I'd once again experience that emotional cocktail of love, devotion, and escapist bliss.

But as move-in day came to a close, and I found myself in a strange house, sitting on a couch that wasn't mine, surrounded by interior decorating choices that weren't mine… that same sensation I'd experienced the morning after my marriage took over. I tried to push it aside, convince myself my life would be perfect now, but I couldn't shake the creeping feeling that all of it was a mistake.

Chapter Five

Any remaining fantasies I had of wedded bliss and companionship never saw fruition. A change came over Donovan after we moved into the house, almost like someone had flipped a switch. He was rarely home, and every night he rolled in far after the sun had set. I blamed most of this on his erratic schedule. The Roadhouse was open until the small hours of the night, and even though the kitchen stopped serving food before midnight, he still had to stay afterward to close up the back and clean. But even on those days when he wasn't on the schedule, he never stuck around. He'd go off somewhere without telling me his plans and was gone all day.

When he was home, he was short with me. If I tried to hold a conversation, he'd either dismiss me or mock me to the point where I fell silent. Often, he'd snap at me, throwing insults and reiterating that, once again, I was too "high and mighty" to do ecstasy with him anymore. He called me "pretentious" and "prudish." The outbursts put me on edge. I started choosing my words carefully to avoid setting him off. He claimed it was stress. I claimed that was bullshit.

Since he'd decided to act this way, I reciprocated. I gave him short answers or pretended not to be interested in what he was saying, even though there was nothing I would have liked more than for us to be as we were before. Once I'd resigned myself to be quieter, he grew talkative again. But he didn't talk *to* me so much as he talked *at* me. He went on and on about his classes, all the literature he was reading and how they thematically connected to one another. Donovan felt everything was connected to everything else. The smallest instance was a grand sign from some great, universal power, and he projected this belief onto his studies.

Sometimes he would show me books from his collection. I recognized the classics, but anything obscure was forgettable to me. I did note he had a number of books on Satanism, though. He had the oddest assortment of works that talked about "sex magic," a set of satanic rituals that utilized sex to control people. I didn't find it nearly as fascinating as he did. Whenever I brought up something I wanted to talk about, I was promptly shut down, or Donovan would suddenly lose interest in our conversation.

I began to grow lonely, and more than that, I was bored. While the occasional outing still sounded like a good time, without Donovan, I had no one around to hang out with. I wasn't one to go out and tackle the great, wide world by myself; if I wasn't out with friends or family, I was content to exist in my own quiet corner. Which was exactly the situation I constantly found myself in. My days were spent in the house, watching TV or reading. Sitting alone in a silent house, doing nothing, feeling neglected—that became my life.

Donovan started cheating on me about a year after the move.

I never confronted him about it, nor did he ever mention his other woman, but my gut told me she was a coworker at the restaurant. It just seemed obvious. When you've been with someone for so long, you just *know*. Even so, bringing it up felt counterproductive. I didn't ask about the hickeys that started to appear on his neck. I didn't ask about her or even what her name was, and I didn't ask how long it'd been going on. Call me a fool, but I gave him the benefit of the doubt and decided it wasn't a serious affair.

As I predicted, he never did anything with that fucking English degree. After graduation, he continued to work as a cook at the Roadhouse. Nothing about that place sat right with me. If we didn't need the money so badly, I would have tried talking Donovan into quitting, or at least applying somewhere else. Granted, I doubted he would have listened to me. He liked the Roadhouse, and he and Tomas appeared to have become colleagues in more than one way.

Just like the cheating, I never brought it up, but something in my gut was telling me Donovan had joined one of Tomas' drug rings. He was making purchases far too expensive to be supported by the wages of a common line cook. Our bills were paid even without the use of my parents' credit card. The only paycheck deposited into our account came from the Roadhouse, so unless customers started tipping their chefs all of a sudden, the only other conclusion I could make was Donovan had begun to deal drugs.

I could see how profitable it was, being we lived so close to a large university. There was always a constant stream of fresh buyers; new kids arrived, bright-eyed and out from under their parents' supervision for the first time—perfect targets for getting hooked on product. I tried not to dwell on that.

It was a tricky position to be in. On the one hand, I had fringe knowledge of a drug ring and a possible "in," while on the other hand, I was in Greenville, potentially benefiting from a less-than-respectable source of income just like a good chunk of the neighborhood was doing. Decidedly, my best course of action was not to say a word. I had no proof, and our financials were stable. My living conditions were solitary and dull, but comfortable. If my husband was involved in illegal activity, the last thing I wanted was to be informed about it. In the end, I kept my silence.

Sadly, I was doomed to discover my involvement with Donovan's newfound lucrative hobby was deeper than I thought.

I was still regularly taking my three prescribed pills: Xanax, Vicodin, and Soma. One for the mind, one for the body, and one for the soul. I never thought to keep track of them, but after a while, I began to notice I was going to the pharmacy more and more frequently to order refills. This was strange, seeing as I only took one of each daily or as needed. I shouldn't have been running out of them as quickly as was, and I never saw Donovan take any of them (and I would've known, being home all the time like I was).

So I started counting my pills. One morning, I opened those little orange bottles one by one and wrote down the amount of doses they held: sixty Xanax, forty Vicodin, and twenty-five Soma. Good numbers to start with. Now all I had to do was keep track and see how fast I was using up each prescription. It felt like a science experiment or a kids' demented math problem—if Ruby has twenty Soma pills on Sunday and fourteen Soma pills on Saturday, how many Soma pills did Ruby take?

During the first week, the numbers decreased at the rate I expected. I'd taken seven Xanax, and the number of Xanax pills in the bottle had been cut by seven. Perfect. It's silly, but I felt proud of this simple accounting system I'd put in place. It gave me an odd sense of control over something, albeit something small. The act of counting pills became part of my daily routine, adding a neat layer of structure and activity into my otherwise monotonous day-to-day. I couldn't rely on Donovan to be around for me, but I could rely on the pills to always add up.

So, naturally, I was completely thrown off when the amount of pills stopped adding up.

It was ten days into my counting project when it happened. According to my handwritten spreadsheet, there should have been fifty Xanax, thirty Vicodin, and fifteen Soma, but each bottle had far less than the predicted amount.

I counted again, assuming I'd missed a few or my mind had blanked on the numbers. Still, everything was off. I counted again and then again and again like an obsessive crazy person. On the fifth round, I started questioning my sanity, but I *knew* the number of pills that should've been there, and with each count I prayed those missing pills would magically appear and put the dumb fucking world back in order. When they didn't, I checked the bottles to make sure I'd poured out their contents entirely. They were empty. Everything they contained was spread out on the kitchen counter, mocking me with their refusal to add up correctly.

My hands gripped the edge of the countertop as I glared down at my small, round assailants. Seething in the height of my frustration, I found myself hating those fucking pills. For years and years, I'd been taking the same set of prescriptions, only for them to vex me so unnecessarily. Damn Donovan for insisting I ask for more pills so frequently. Half of me wondered if I even needed them anymore; the other half—a very spiteful half—agreed. So I said fuck it.

Sweeping them all into my hand, I marched to the bathroom and aggressively flipped up the toilet seat. I watched the myriad of pills cascade from my palm into the porcelain bowl and didn't hesitate for a moment to flush them all down. The bottles were disposed in the small garbage can next to the toilet.

The deed was done.

As I settled myself in the living room, an odd feeling of freedom washed over me, like I'd suddenly been severed from a ball and chain slowing me down. My chin lifted as I grew more and more satisfied with my decision. I'd cut myself off from my prescriptions for good, and I found a sense of power in the act, more so than I had counting them. Yes, I decided as I flipped on the TV, this was a good move.

Then Donovan came home.

He said nothing to me—he rarely did—just tossed a set of keys on the table and made a beeline for the bathroom to take his usual shower. While I tried to ignore him and keep my eyes on the screen, my gaze habitually flitted toward him in some vain hope of receiving attention and acknowledgement. I ended up receiving both, but not in the way I wanted.

From the bathroom, Donovan gave a cry of distress before storming out into the living room. He planted himself in front of the TV, looming over me.

"Where are the pills?" he asked forcefully.

"What about them?" I shot back.

"The *pills*," he repeated. "Your fucking prescriptions—where are they?"

I shrugged. "I flushed them down the toilet."

His face contorted with fury and irritation. "You *what*?"

It was frustrating when I couldn't hold back the flinch. He'd raised his voice at me before, but this decibel was a new high. I tried to match it while staying calm. "I flushed them—"

"No, I heard you. What the fuck got in your head to make you think that was a good idea?" He clenched his fists and paced around the living room.

"What? They were mine."

"You have no idea what you've just done!" he shouted, completely steamrolling over my words. Running his fingers through his hair, he approached me again, this time leaning against the armrest so his face was inches from mine. He spoke low and through gritted teeth. "If you had just kept taking your pills and kept your head under the covers, everything would have been fine."

Before I could respond, Donovan moved away and snatched up his keys. I heard the stomping of his shoes move to the front door, then a forceful slam as he left the house.

I remained shaking in my seat, feeling unnerved from the confrontation, but also strangely guilty and sad. Longing creeped in amid the cocktail of emotions. Those early days of escape and ecstasy danced in my head like distant memories. I tried to picture the Donovan I met at that party long ago treating me the way *this* Donovan did just then. It was hard to picture them as the same person. Impossible, even. Yet they were the same—confusingly, they were the same. I loved old Donovan and feared new Donovan, and my mind struggled to reconcile them as the same person. Damn it all.

When I found the energy to stand, I rushed to the kitchen to pour myself a drink. Three vodka shots in, I started to calm down and reclaim some sense of clarity. Tipsy but at ease, I tried to reason why it was so damn important for Donovan that I have my pills.

The reason was so obvious and so simple, I nearly kicked myself for not figuring it out before. Donovan had been the one to insist on my prescription refills, and given all my suspicions about his "business" with Tomas...

Shit.

Shit, shit, *shit*!

I downed another shot of vodka, furious that I'd let myself be strung along as an unwitting drug supplier. Well, now there was no *way* I could say something. How the fuck was I supposed to explain my part in this as ignorance? "I'm sorry, officer. My husband simply *insisted* I get more and more refills. I just seemed to be going through my pills so fast—it's such a mystery!" No. Absolutely not.

Later, when I'd sobered up, I tried to take solace in the fact that I'd cut off Donovan's supply indefinitely. If all my suspicions were correct, and he *had* been selling my pills on the street, then there was one less source of product for him to acquire inventory. Maybe he'd even struggle to find a replacement and business would crumble. Maybe he'd grow frustrated and bow out. Even better, maybe Tomas would drop him like a stone. I could only hope.

* * *

A couple months later, I took a day to rearrange some things in the house. The desk we kept in the living room was loaded with papers, and I took it on as a project to organize everything. As I emptied one drawer, I noticed it was much shallower than the others, even though they were supposed to be uniform in size. After a quick inspection, I found a small indent that acted as a makeshift handle. I hooked my fingernail underneath in and lifted. What lay inside that secret compartment made me gasp.

Staring me in the face was a fat envelope stuffed to the brim with cash. My hand instinctively reached for it before I stopped, thinking better of it. Even though I was home alone, I did a quick scan of my surroundings to be sure, then hastily replaced the lid and stuffed the papers back in the drawer. I mussed up the rest of the desk, making sure to put everything back *exactly* the way I found it.

As I finished my task, my hands trembled. There were no longer any doubts about Donovan's activity. I'd stumbled across all the proof I needed, and the revelation shook me to my core. Once again, I found myself reaching for the vodka bottle, and for the rest of the night I busied myself by liberating it of its contents.

Despite all my efforts to calm my nerves, I couldn't kill the anxiety telling me Donovan would suss out my discovery when he got home. Thankfully, he didn't. He merely stumbled through the door and proceeded to ignore me as usual. I'd never been so relieved to be invisible to a person.

Still, the money never completely left my mind. There was no way I'd go back to count it—I *knew* Donovan would find out I'd uncovered his stash and go after me—but based on the number of zeros on those bills, I estimated there were at least a hundred thousand dollars in that drawer.

Chapter Six

There was only so much loneliness I could take. I craved affection and attention desperately like I never had before. So, I did what a lot of lonely people do: I got a dog.

Well, I *eventually* got a dog. Donovan wasn't on board with the idea at first, and it didn't feel right to move forward with the process without his approval. After all, it would be his dog too even if I promised to take care of it. After days of bringing up the subject to him, he finally agreed to the idea, but only on the stipulation that he could name the dog. I was so desperate for a companion, I didn't give a shit by that point. I told him that was fine.

The search for the perfect dog didn't take long, as I fell in love with a puppy almost right away. I found a shelter with a litter of beautiful American Eskimo Dogs, and they were old enough to go to a good home. One of the puppies took to me immediately, and I brought her home to present her to Donovan. He commented about how much he liked her white fur and seemed to have a name in mind from the moment I brought her through the door.

"Her name will be Lucy," he stated authoritatively, "after Lucifer."

I grimaced, not super thrilled to have this playful little angel of a puppy earn her moniker from the Devil himself. Donovan noticed my distain for the name choice.

"This was the deal, Ruby," he reminded me.

"I know, I know," I said, holding my hand out to... *Lucy*. She padded up to me to receive head scratches. "Lucy's fine."

Lucy was more than fine, actually. She was perfect. Having her around seemed to brighten up the house and lift my spirits. Raising her gave me a better sense of purpose than counting those fucking pills did. I let myself get lost in teaching her tricks, taking her for walks, and playing fetch. Getting her potty trained was a pain in the ass, but even when she had accidents in the house and I had to get on my hands and knees to clean it up, I couldn't stay mad at her. No matter how bad my day was, she was always happy to see me. It was a validation I hadn't experienced in a long time.

I was more than glad for Lucy's company, given Donovan's continual avoidance of me. He seemed to have gotten it in his head that if I had my dog, then he *really* didn't need to be around. It seemed I saw him less and less, and on those rare days he offered to do something with me, I eagerly stuck to him. While we didn't have the best marriage, I still found myself wanting to make things work. I kept searching for ways to make him smile, happy, or simply notice me. His attention was all I wanted, and the more he denied me, the greater my longing grew.

One night, on one of Donovan's rare days off, he invited me out to dinner at the Roadhouse. As uncomfortable as the place made me feel, I was elated for the promise of quality time together. I dolled myself up, wanting to look my best on this rare occasion, then we were out the door.

The restaurant was hopping that night. Bodies packed the bar, and every booth was filled with regulars and people who were bound to become regulars. Even though the wait time was long, the hostess seemed find a table for us pretty quickly. The swift service didn't sway me much from the comment she made about me, though. The moment we approached her podium, she looked me up and down, turned to Donovan, and said, "I see she finally let you out of your cage."

Donovan chuckled in some agreement, but I recoiled, taken totally aback by this comment. *His* cage? The man who stayed out at all hours and did whatever he pleased and probably kept a thousand secrets—yes. I was the one certainly holding him back.

The tone of her speech irked me too. Maybe if she'd said it playfully, it wouldn't have bothered me so, but it was so aggressive—*disdainful*—like she already had a picture of who I was (or supposedly was) in her head. I eyed Donovan as we were ushered to our table, wondering what, exactly, he'd been saying to his coworkers about me.

Throughout our meal, other employees of the Roadhouse stopped by to say hi to Donovan. They rarely spoke to me, and when they did it was curt and short. A few shot me dirty looks, and I became more convinced Donovan had gone out of his way to paint me in a bad light to these people. If I didn't know any better, I'd say they were under the impression I was some sort of commanding freeloader. What the hell could he have possibly said to them?

Their judgmental glares made it difficult for me to enjoy my food, and I ended up leaving most of my meal on the plate. As the night wore on, I wanted less and less to be there. I wanted to go home where I felt safe instead of sitting here, surrounded by people who thought ill of me.

Of course, Donovan noticed my discomfort.

"Something wrong?" he asked, though by his smirk I wondered if he already figured it out.

"Nothing," I lied. "Guess I'm just a little tired."

He frowned. "Well, I was hoping we'd enjoy a nice night out since we never do anything together, but if you want to leave…"

"It's fine," I said, another lie. A nagging voice in the back of my head begged for me to stay, and it overwhelmed my discomfort. God only knew when I'd get another chance to go out with Donovan. "I could use the activity."

He smiled and raised his beer in my direction as a toast of thanks. I couldn't help but smile back. Those small moments of togetherness were so important; I had to savor them no matter how badly I wanted to leave that place. Even if he was the cause of it all, I wanted nothing more than to be happy with him.

Yet those constant, judging stares made it difficult for me to enjoy myself.

* * *

In November of 2011, an opportunity cropped up that promised to change things for the better. A university food services department offered Donovan a chef position that paid a thirty-thousand-dollar salary, which was scheduled to begin a couple of months later in January. It came with benefits, too—paid time off, health insurance, the works. He'd also have a regular nine-to-five work schedule, meaning those late nights at the Roadhouse would be far behind us.

When he took the job, I was overjoyed. Finally, he'd have a more open schedule and time to be home in the evenings. Visions of mending our relationship and rekindling that spark we had years ago made me practically float with joy. This was it, I was sure of it. This was the change that would fix everything.

Donovan was even more proud of himself than I was. He boasted for days about his new position, how he had finally "made it" in the world. He even reiterated that silly sentiment he expressed on the night we met about chefs, how they're the most powerful people in the world because they "control what people eat." He started walking around the house with his head held higher, and he spoke louder and more frequently than he used to. The way he acted, you'd think he was just elected governor or something. While the overconfidence got a little grating, I hoped this improved attitude of his would contribute to us being on friendlier terms again.

As 2011 drew to a close, Donovan put his two weeks in at the Roadhouse. Imagine my disappointment when, after his first shift at the new job, he didn't come home. I waited by the door for the first hour, wondering if he'd stopped by the grocery store or something and was just running late. As the minutes ticked on into hours, disappointment seeped its way into my chest. He wasn't coming home on time. He was out doing whatever the hell he'd been doing these last few years. I pictured him out with Tomas, drinking at the Roadhouse or partaking in whatever shady activity they were prone to do.

Giving in, I sat alone and flipped on the TV. Lucy padded over and joined me on the couch—my perfect but only companion. Nothing had changed, and it looked like it was just me and the dog from here on out.

Chapter Seven

B y that point, I'd resigned myself to thinking I was essentially going to spend the rest of my marriage alone. I had my family to visit and the occasional friend to talk to, but outside of Lucy, my home life consisted of little social interaction. Donovan and I weren't even sleeping in the same bed anymore. We'd split off into different bedrooms, adding physical distance to our emotional gap. I never asked about his day; he never asked about mine. We were married on paper, but roommates in practice.

Then, one day, Donovan genuinely surprised me. I was home alone, prepping a light dinner for myself, when I got a phone call from him.

"Hey, are you free later this afternoon?"

I blinked, surprised at the question. "Uh, yes. I am. Why?"

"I'm planning to buy a plot at a community garden in town," he explained. "I want you to come with me to make the purchase."

At first, I didn't know what to say. He'd never expressed interest in gardening before; why now? Maybe it was better not to question it—he just asked me to be part of something with him. I'd take that.

I drove to the garden office and found Donovan waiting in the parking lot for me. He ushered me inside and approached the front desk about purchasing our new plot. I let my eyes wander around the cramped, cluttered office, taking in my new surroundings. On the wall was a sky view picture of the community gardens, sectioned off with red lines to denote who owned what. Donovan came up from behind me to point out a rectangular plot in the back corner of the garden.

"That one's ours," he said. "It's a good spot. Tomas pulled a few strings to hook us up."

I winced at the mention of Tomas's name but nodded in approval and said, "Looks nice and spacious. We'll have to grow tomatoes."

"Yep, that's what I'm thinking too. Peppers, peas, tomatoes, whatever we want." The casual, affectionate way he spoke filled a void.

The guy at the front desk explained the benefits of owning a plot here. Basically, we owned our corner of land, but could only grow what was allowed in the garden (no magnolia trees, for instance, only vegetables and herbs). We were in charge of tending to our own plants, and no one was allowed to work in someone else's plot without their permission. It was also our responsibility to ensure nothing overlapped into another garden—couldn't have a rogue zucchini vine choking the neighbor's basil patch.

Once the paperwork was signed and Donovan and I paid the man, we ventured outside to view our new garden plot. Given it was February, the ground was still blanketed with old, crystalized snow that had mixed messily with the mud around it. The plot didn't look like much, just a flat, brown and white rectangle large enough to fit about two queen-size mattresses. I tried to picture how it would look in June or July, filled to the brim with splendorous green and growing veggies. I liked how tucked away it was in back corner; it seemed quaint and cozy, and that brought on a fuzzy feeling inside me.

Donovan wasted no time marching around the plot and motioning to its different sections, audibly mapping out what would be planted where. I joined him, nodding at his suggestions to keep the tomatoes and peppers separated and occasionally adding my own two cents. In that moment, we were a team again. Gardens were hard work, I knew that, but this was something Donovan wanted us to do together. Despite everything my husband had become, it felt like the plot had brought him back to me. Maybe this was his way of trying to reconcile things. I silently promised to work my ass off and make him see what we could still sow together.

* * *

It was far too cold to start breaking up the garden's soil, and after doing some light research, I found we couldn't plant anything until late April or May to keep the seeds safe from the frost. The rest of February was then spent planning and prepping the layout of our plot and what we'd grow in it. The idea was to buy some ready-to-plant vegetables for tomatoes and bell peppers; that was easier than growing something straight from seed. Everything else, we'd try our luck starting them from scratch.

In mid-March, most of the snow melted and the temperatures rose. It became a waiting game for sunshine as rain kept pouring and pouring down. Every morning, I'd check the weather and be disappointed to see signs of scattered showers. Watching TV, I'd occasionally glance out the window and scowl at the raindrops hitting the pane. I imagined they were mocking me.

Impatient as I was to get outside and work in the garden with Donovan, there was nothing we could do about the weather, and so we let the days go by as usual.

"Tomas is coming over," Donovan said one day at breakfast. He'd begun cooking for us again, which I saw as a good sign. If he was doing nice things for me, that told me we were one step closer to loving each other again. Although it didn't help that this lovely meal he'd prepared was being soiled by Tomas.

"What for?" I asked with more bite than I planned.

"He just got back from visiting family in Panama," he explained. "I asked him to bring home some special seeds for me. He's dropping them off."

My brow furrowed in confusion. "What special seeds?"

"Just something from his home country I wanted," he said simply. As if to punctuate the statement, he stood, washed his plate, and exited the kitchen without any elaboration.

Left alone at the table, I tried to reason out what on earth Donovan could want from Panama. Assuming this was for the vegetable garden, it could've been some local produce not found in the US. But then why be coy about it? The phrase "special seeds" made it sound like weed, but no one had to go all the way to Central America to find that.

Whatever it was, both Donovan and Tomas seemed to go out of their way to make sure I didn't hear the plant's name. When Tomas arrived, he only referred to his delivery with the same phrase, saying, "Here're those special seeds you wanted." Donovan thanked him, and I waited for them to start discussing the seeds—their name, how to grow them, or anything about them, really. Instead, Donovan veered the conversation to Tomas's trip to Panama. Neither acknowledged me, and I eventually left for my bedroom to be alone.

A few more days of gloomy March later, the weather finally let up, giving us some sunshine and warmth to work in the plot. I was looking forward to a day of gardening with Donovan, picturing it as productive, quality time together. When I got in the car, I noticed he didn't pack any gardening tools. I'd expected a hoe or at least a shovel, but no. He brought nothing. I shrugged it off, assuming the community garden would have tools available.

We must have been the early birds because there was no one else working in their plot that day. I was fine with that—all the better to bond with my husband.

Standing with our hands on our hips, we surveyed the work-in-progress that was our new garden. It was still damp from all the rain and the melted snow, but I could see the soil looked rich and dark. The smell of the wet earth was almost pleasant.

"First thing is to break up the dirt," Donovan said. "If we dig all the rocks out, that should do the trick."

I nodded and looked at him, waiting for him to fetch a rake or something, or at least a pair of gloves. Instead, he stared at me, then inclined his head to the plot. He spoke casually, but with a slight air of authority laced in. "Go on, get started."

My face was as indignant as it could possibly be. "Uh… Sorry, what?" What he was asking was ridiculous. Get on my hands and knees and dig in the dirt without any gloves or tools—what the fuck? I had to be sure I understood.

"We need to pick out the rocks," he repeated. "Go on."

He was serious.

I regarded him for a single, defiant moment before I gingerly knelt down and reached for a loose rock nestled in the soil. Plucking it up, I glanced at Donovan to make triply sure he wasn't kidding around. The intent on his face told me he wasn't.

"Now throw it away," he said, as though I couldn't comprehend this simple task.

I tossed it aside, and Donovan's eyes flicked toward the ground, telling me to keep going. A flushed embarrassment smeared itself across my face. There was an urge to stand up and tell him to fuck off, that if he wanted the rocks gone so badly, he could get down on his own knees and do it himself. The moment played out in my mind vividly, but my body veered toward compliance. It moved mechanically and purposefully, like it didn't have a choice but to complete the task at hand. Soon my hands were caked in wet earth as I dug around, picking stone after stone from their bed and flinging them to the grass.

As much as I tried to keep myself and my clothes clean, the ground was still wet from all the rain, which made it cling to my skin and find its way onto everything I wore. My shoes were stained brown, and damp soil built up on my knees. No matter how many times I dug the dirt from under my fingernails, more would immediately take its place. I felt disgusting.

All the while, Donovan continued to watch me. It was eerie how silent he was. I could just picture how he looked behind my back—looming, staring, observing. He never made a sound. Didn't move or go to fetch anything to help work the soil. He just watched. Knowing he was surveying my every movement made them feel sluggish and heavy. The hate and degradation that coursed through my veins combated against the idiotic desire to do the job and do the job well. An inkling nestled in the back of my mind, telling me if I did this, our relationship would be mended or righted somehow. The more sober part of me shoved those thoughts aside, and I let all the anger I wanted to feel saturate my bones. *Fuck* Donovan, and fuck these goddamn rocks and the dirt and all the rain that made it muddy. Fuck *everything*.

It all got worse when Tomas arrived.

The sight of his car parking in the lot made my heart sink. It was bad enough Donovan was watching me like this; I didn't want anyone else to see me in this state. Tomas approached, greeting Donovan and not saying a word to me at all. Fine by me—I didn't want to talk to him or anyone else while I was on my knees and covered in mud.

After their quick exchange, things went quiet again. Goosebumps washed over my skin in waves as I imaged what was happening. As I tossed a particularly large rock aside, I risked a glance behind me and confirmed my sick suspicion. They were both watching me now. Side by side and silent like the Grady twins from *The Shining*. But instead of asking me to play with them, they were content to look down on me as I dug around in the fucking dirt.

Bile threatened to rise in my throat. Unnerved didn't even begin to describe the discomfort I felt. I wanted nothing more than to get up and run all the way back to my house, where a warm shower and the vodka bottle would be waiting in welcome. Yet, their stares cemented me in place, rooting me to the ground and daring me not to stand up until I had picked every single rock out of that garden plot.

The more I worked, the sicker I was of staring at soil, so I started to let my eyes wander to get a glimpse of the sky and my surroundings. That's when I spotted a sign located on the fence surrounding the garden. It was an advertisement announcing rototills for rent. Seeing it gave me pause, and for the first time I broke my monotonous pattern of grasping rocks and tossing them. Glancing back at Donovan, I inclined my hand toward the sign.

"Did you see that?" I asked. "If we got a rototill, it'd be much quicker than digging the rocks out ourselves." *Ourselves.* More like *myself.*

Donovan followed my pointed finger to the sign and merely shrugged. "I've already put in an order to rent one."

I whipped my head back at him. "What!?"

"I've got it reserved for next week."

My mouth hung agape, totally speechless and incredulous. What the hell had been the point of making me do this if he was just going to turn up the dirt himself?

He regarded me indifferently, ignoring my shock at the revelation. "Are you almost done?" he asked. Beside him, Tomas continued to watch on with silent apathy. Something about his presence discouraged me from making a scene.

I clenched my jaw, furious at the both of them, but I felt powerless to just walk away from the situation. With a short, tight response of, "Yes," I turned back to the ground and resumed my duty.

It took me another hour to get it all done.

Chapter Eight

Donovan, thankfully, never again asked me to work in the garden alone. I'd been too humiliated by the event to bring it up to anyone, which left me alone to stew in my own bitterness. After enough time passed, I was able to simmer down from the initial bought of anger and try to find the silver lining, wherever it could be. Donovan and I still had a garden to tend, and we'd be doing it together.

From then on, our time out in the plot was normal. No strange, one-sided acts of labor, just two people prepping a square of earth for planting, using tools like *proper* gardeners.

Still, I couldn't shake the dreadful feeling that came over me whenever I thought back to that day in the dirt. It had been so weird and unsettling—I would damn near call it cult-like. Tomas was a sick fuck, that much was clear, but whatever Donovan's intention was for that day, I doubted I'd ever figure it out. Visiting the plot after he had taken the rototill through it put a bad taste in my mouth. The machine had done its work so perfectly, it basically rendered all my efforts pointless.

We continued to work on the garden together, though, so even if I couldn't entirely shake the event from my mind, being a part of *something* made it easier to put on the backburner.

I wished I could say the garden brought us closer together, but outside those days of agrarian labor, things more or less remained the same. Donovan still stayed out till all hours, even when he wasn't working. In fact, on top of his new salary position with the university, he still picked up shifts at the Roadhouse in the evenings. I couldn't say why. It wasn't like we were hurting for money. I thought of that envelope of cash sitting in the drawer and wondered if it was still there or if it'd been spent or moved. I was too timid to check.

The one major change that became a constant was the way Donovan kept up his new habit of cooking us dinner. While preparing our meals, he'd brag about his skills as a chef and how important his position at the restaurant was. I let him have it, nodding in agreement to humor him. Being a chef was a good job, don't get me wrong, but I doubted being employed at university food services in a small town was the grand, pretentious profession he made it out to be.

One thing was for sure, though: the food he made was fucking good. As grating as his boasting could get, he'd hear no complaints from me.

Since Donovan was still gone for most of the time, I was again left to spend my free time alone with Lucy. She remained a decent replacement for human interaction, even if I missed the basic social practice of simple conversation. I made up for it by talking to the dog, asking her questions like, "Alright, what should it be today, Lucy, vodka or beer?" as if she'd understand and respond. The replies I usually got consisted of her sitting pretty with her tail wagging as she begged for treats.

Donovan and I looked into getting cats, and I was more than welcome to introduce more pets into the household. We adopted two, and this time I was allowed to name them: Mokie and Twizzler. They were sweet cats, and Lucy got along with them well enough considering the eternal rivalry between cats and dogs. Having all three of them in the house with me made the place feel less isolating and secluded when I was left alone.

One on of the rare days Donovan decided to stay home, I heard him conversing with Lucy in the kitchen. I entered to refill my water glass and saw he was hand feeding her grapes. I knew how poisonous those could be to dogs, and the sight of what he was doing nearly sent me into a fit. The loud gasp that burst from my mouth alerted him, and he looked up.

"What are you doing? Stop!" I yelled, tearing the grapes from his hand.

He gave me a perturbed expression and shrugged. "I'm just giving her a treat."

"Dogs can't eat grapes!" I exclaimed. "They're poisonous for them! You could give her a UTI."

Lucy, for her part, sat between the two of us, wagging her tail and letting her eyes follow the grapes in my hands as I waved them about in frustration.

"Fine," he scoffed. The way he spoke gave me the impression he didn't see the harm in what he'd done. "I won't do it again."

"Hell no, you won't! The last thing I need is my dog dying on me."

"The dog's not going to die. I didn't give her that many," he insisted.

That didn't stop me from worrying. I kept a sharp eye on Lucy for the rest of the day to spot any signs of illness. She seemed fine, behavior wise, and by the end of the day I convinced myself she'd be okay.

As the week went on, I noticed Lucy started asking to go outside more frequently to pee. Her whine at the door sounded pleading and more urgent. After she begged for five pee breaks in the span of an hour, I grew too concerned to ignore what could be happening. I called Donovan and told him I was taking Lucy to an emergency vet visit.

"Right now?" he asked.

"Yeah."

"Okay, I'll meet you there."

That was a shocker. Donovan had never taken interest in the dog like that before. He especially had never gone with me to a vet appointment.

Sure enough, as I sat in the waiting room with Lucy lying pitifully on my lap, Donovan burst through the door and planted himself next to me. I nearly asked why he'd decided to come, but I chalked it up as an assumption that maybe he was really worried about the dog and wanted to be here. Maybe he felt guilty about the grapes or something.

One of the assistants called us into a room, and she and the vet performed a thorough check on Lucy. I stood to the side, nervously tapping my fingernails against my chin. Donovan remained stoic, almost disinterested.

When I explained her frequent urination, they told me they would need to extract a urine sample. I tensed up at the sight of the needle, and even though the assistant soothed Lucy with pets and calming words, it didn't stop me from flinching when the pointed tip broke skin. I stayed with Lucy as they performed tests on the sample. She looked at me with big, shiny eyes as I petted her head and told her what a good girl she was, that everything would be fine.

The moment the vet told us my dog had a UTI, I knew immediately it was because of the grapes. I didn't say anything, wanting to save that conversation for when Donovan and I got home. Luckily, we'd caught the infection fast enough that it could be easily treated with a round of antibiotics. The vet left the room, saying his assistant would return with the medication and our bill. It was relieving to know Lucy would be fine.

Once we were alone in the room, Donovan nudged me to get my attention. He drew me to a poster hanging on the wall. It depicted the number of foods found to be harmful to dogs. He was pointing to one food in particular: grapes.

I was about to tell him yes, of course grapes were bad—we'd already gone over this, but the words stayed in my mouth when I noticed his expression. His face was contorted into a grin so wide it looked inhumane. Devilish, even. A cruel self-satisfaction seemed to emanate from him, and I wracked my brain trying to figure out what he was communicating here.

He said not a word, and neither did I. I chose to ignore him, trying instead to hold my attention on my whining dog laying on the table.

Even long after things were said and done and Lucy got better, I couldn't shake the image of Donovan's knowing, maniacal face from my mind.

Chapter Nine

Those "special seeds" Tomas gifted to Donovan remained a mystery to me. Donovan never referred to them by name, and whenever we discussed what we needed to do for the garden, he conveniently seemed to leave them out of the conversation. It was apparent he meant for them to be planted in our plot, though. I saw him in the garage filling seed trays with soil and dropping a seed into each of the wells.

When I asked about it, he just said it was one of those plants you had to start growing indoors before they could go in the ground. Something about a difference in climate between Central America and where we lived. Made sense to me, and I was glad he explained at least that much about them.

I assumed he planned to keep the seedlings in the garage until the weather warmed up enough for them to be moved to the garden. And for a time, he did. Then, one day, I entered the living room and found them covering my desk. By that point, Donovan had transplanted them into individual plastic pots, and they populated every inch of surface, crowding out anything I'd placed there. Bits of dirt dotted the wood, and I noticed some water had leaked through the bottoms of the pots and soaked into some of my papers and books.

My lips pursed at the sight. Turning heel, I prepared myself to call out Donovan on what he'd done and ask why the hell he'd decided to invade my space like this. When I found him in the kitchen cutting vegetables, he looked up and spoke before I got a word out.

"Those need to go outside," he stated plainly. "They need direct sunlight."

The statement threw me so off guard, I spluttered in trying to form a retort. I wanted to demand he explain his actions—why bother moving them into the house if they needed to be outside? And why *my* fucking desk when literally any other spot was available? In the end, my thoughts coalesced into, "Why don't *you* do it?"

"I'm busy. Don't you want a nice dinner?" His words were frustratingly casual and simple, punctuated by the knife he held forcefully slicing through a carrot and loudly smacking the cutting board.

Rolling my eyes, I made a sound that landed somewhere between a sigh and a groan and stormed back to the living room. I glared down at those damn seedlings, bitter about the task I'd been assigned. It didn't feel as degrading as picking stones from the dirt, but the request had that same unnecessary air to it. The garden was his idea. These fucking *seeds* were his idea. If he wanted this done so badly, why bother with the extra step of having me do it? The speed at which I carried the pots out to the yard seemed to be fueled by spite alone.

It took six trips.

* * *

At last, the weather warmed up to a point where we were past any danger of frost, and we were able to plant our vegetables. After a day's worth of work, we had a modest number of corn, bell peppers, tomatoes, zucchini, and carrots all snug in the ground. The "special" seedlings were planted in the far corner of the plot, positioned so they bordered no one else's garden. Beforehand, Donovan had asked me with increasing frequency to take them outside, to the point where it had almost become a daily chore. I was glad to see them planted; no more menial back-and-forth from the house to the yard for me.

Again, I was filled with the urge to ask Donovan what the hell they were, but given how secretive he was about them, part of me felt it was best not to pry.

I decided to keep silent about the mystery plant. The rest of the garden, the part we would work on *together*, was more important to me than those stupid seeds.

We'd purchased the pepper and tomato seedlings from a local greenhouse, but the corn, zucchini, and carrots were planted as seeds. Within a week, the first bits of green began to peek out of the ground, and before long, baby leaves beautifully carpeted the plot. There was a strange satisfaction in watching everything grow. It was simple and sublime and appealed to that lonely side of me that sought a happy, peaceful life free of stress and drama. Even though I'd come home sweaty and filthy and in desperate want of a shower, I found I enjoyed working in the garden and wanted to ensure it succeeded.

So, of course, while we were busy weeding one morning, I had to bring up the fact that Donovan hadn't staked the tomatoes yet.

"I read you're supposed to do it when they're first planted," I said. "If you wait too long, it might damage the roots."

"They'll be fine," he responded, not looking up from the stinging nettle he was digging up with a hoe.

I blinked, frustrated at the blind dismissal of my concern. Not wanting this mistake to be overlooked, I pushed the issue further. "I'm pretty sure when they get bigger, they'll get too top-heavy and fall over."

"I said they'll be fine," he insisted. There was a hint of annoyance there.

Well, that made two of us. The heat rose to my face as I grew increasingly more convinced that I was right, and he should listen to me. But I didn't want to argue, not here. Not in the only place we'd found any common ground in our recent years of marriage.

I stood and brushed the excess dirt from my hands. Making up a quick lie about getting a drink of water, I sauntered away and found a place in the shade, out of sight from our plot. I leaned against the community garden's office building, appreciating the coolness of its bricks on my back.

I was right. I *knew* I was right. Tomato plants had to be staked; that's just how you grow tomatoes. So why wasn't he listening? Because I'd brought it up and not him? What the fuck sort of logic was that?

For not the first time, I wondered why I was here. Not in Greenville or out in the garden, but with Donovan. The sequence of events that brought us together felt so serendipitous at the time. If only the follow-up had been just as enchanting. For years, it'd been like this: his word was just, my word was wrong, and how dare I offer my input on anything. We were distant, argumentative, and yet I longed for things to work between us. Time and time again, I'd wished for things to revert back to those weekend getaways in his apartment, waiting for us to fall in love again, thinking maybe *this* time I'd be happy. And was I happy?

No.

And I wasn't sure if I'd be willing to wait around much longer.

As I idly watched the cars go by—arms crossed, fingers drumming—I let myself breathe and contemplate and stew in my bitter thoughts and nostalgia.

Chapter Ten

It was mid-June when I started to feel sick.

I woke up one morning to a bad bought of nausea and immediately decided to take it easy for the day. Hunger evaded me, and food sounded disgusting anyway, so I sipped some water and popped something to help my stomach settle before crawling back into bed. I remained there until the sun was close to setting, getting up only when Lucy whined to go outside or when Twizzler's obnoxious prodding told me he needed to be fed.

On top of the nausea, my head was pounding. It was one of the most piercing headaches I'd ever experienced, and I couldn't shake it, no matter how much Ibuprofen I took.

Exhaustion overtook me. My muscles felt weak, and when I did stand up, it took monumental effort. Still, I couldn't sleep. I wanted to, but the dull pain in my gut refused to let my mind rest. I tossed and turned in agony, too tired to get up but too restless to sleep. For a moment, I almost contemplated downing a shot of vodka to knock me out, but I'd more than likely just throw it right back up.

When Donovan got home from work, he found me still in bed. Standing in my doorway, he shook his head at me and said, "Guess you had a lazy day while I was out working."

Spite encouraged me to swivel around so I could face him and give him the dirtiest look I could muster. I was so not in the mood.

"I feel like shit," I said shortly. "Just leave me alone."

He tutted. "Touchy. Well, sleep it off, I guess."

"Working on it," I spat bitterly before rolling away to face the wall. I didn't hear his footsteps leave for a long while.

* * *

Though the nausea lingered the next day, I felt well enough to get out of bed and do things around the house. My stomach complained loudly from going a whole day without food, and I satisfied it with some lightly salted crackers and fruit. I took Lucy for a walk, and the fresh air was rejuvenating. My strength had recovered to the point where I didn't feel the need to lay down and rest. Even the dinner Donovan cooked for us that night was appetizing enough for me to eat. Whatever bug I'd caught, my body must've been fighting it off just fine.

The day after, however, I felt like shit again.

It wasn't as bad as that first day; I could get out of bed, at the very least. If I occupied my mind enough, I could almost ignore the nausea, but if I stood up after sitting down for too long, it'd kick into high gear. Or, if I moved too fast, a piercing pain would pinch my forehead. Food seemed like my enemy, but I managed to get down some toast, and I made sure to regularly sip on a glass of water.

Over the course of a week, the on-and-off nausea persisted, coupled with the purgatory of exhaustion and the inability to sleep. It became a vicious cycle of feeling hungry, but not wanting to eat and feeling tired, but not sleeping. Some days, it grew so bad I was all but useless. I didn't take care of the animals, or go out in the garden, or even so much as dress myself. I made sure to take advantage of the times when I had enough strength to do all those things. Unfortunately, that only exhausted me more.

I tried to reason out what it could be. Mono? The flu? A migraine? Any seemed likely, though that last one seemed like it aligned the most with what I was feeling. At least, it did until I started experiencing other symptoms I couldn't explain.

At night, when I couldn't sleep, I could've sworn I heard *noises*. They varied in type and intensity: scratches, voices, whistles, all sounding right beside my ear, as if some invisible being was haunting my pillow. The quiet ones unnerved me, and the loud ones startled me into squealing with fright. I blamed it on the animals at first, but the sounds were too close and would occur whether Lucy or the cats were in the room with me or not.

I attempted to hunt down a source. There had to be something in my room making all this noise. I checked the vents, the fan, even my TV. I unplugged every electronic and turned off my phone, and still I heard noises. They were infrequent and vague, and some nights I never heard anything, but they were there.

One morning at breakfast, as I was fighting off a headache and what had become my usual queasiness, I asked Donovan if he was hearing anything at night.

"No, I haven't," he replied. "What are you hearing?"

I tried to articulate as best I could. "Like scraping sounds, or like someone's trying to talk to me, but it's all muffled. I don't know, just noises."

"Might be a raccoon outside," he suggested.

"Hmm, maybe."

"Or maybe you're just tired."

It made sense. It didn't account for everything, but it made sense. Maybe my lack of sleep was causing my brain to play tricks on me. Daydreaming, but on another level.

Yes, that was it, I decided. I wasn't feeling well, and I wasn't sleeping, so my brain was glitching and making me hear noises. That had to be it. Once I got better, they'd go away.

It was wishful thinking.

I didn't get better, not by a long shot. In fact, I got worse and started to experience even more symptoms. Strange bruises started to appear on my legs, dotting my skin with purple splotches that pained me when I poked them. Clumps of my hair began to fall out. I'd take a shower and find clods of it clogging up the drain.

When I did feel well enough to leave the house, I made an appointment with my hair dresser to try to clean things up a little. As she worked on my mess, she made the strangest comment.

"Are you pregnant?" she asked.

It was so out of the blue; I was taken aback for a moment before I could respond.

"No?" I said, letting my confusion be known. "Why?"

"You've got some acne on your scalp, and it looks oily," she explained. "Normally, I only see it this bad from pregnant women."

"Oh... No, I'm definitely not. There's no way." It was impossible, really. Donovan and I had stopped having sex ages ago.

She nodded, running her fingers through my hair and frowning when a chunk of it came away. "I'll massage in some moisturizer. That should help. We've got a couple shampoos on the shelf for thinning hair, if you're interested."

Lost in my thoughts and worries, I mechanically thanked her and told her yes, I'd look at the shampoos. Paranoia seeped in, convincing me the chance of pregnancy was low but not zero. Fuck me, my mind even thought back to the plot of *Rosemary's Baby*.

I had to know for sure.

When I left the salon, I made a beeline for the drug store, purchased a pack of two tests, and took them both in the store's public bathroom. They were negative. Of course they were.

It was still a relief.

That wasn't the end of it, though. Glancing in the mirror one morning, I noticed my face was red. Beet red like I'd been laying in the sun for too long and burned it. But I hadn't been outside much, not with how sick I'd been feeling. I checked my temperature. It was at a normal level. I didn't feel warm. My face had just reddened up like a fucking tomato.

When Donovan noticed, he had the same initial instinct I did and asked if I was running a fever. I told him no, my face was just red.

"Weird. You might be having an allergic reaction to something," he offered.

I shrugged. "I've barely gone outside. What would it even be?"

"Sometimes people develop allergies over time." Then, pivoting the conversation entirely, he said, "Oh, I told some of the people at work about the noises you've been hearing."

If my face hadn't already been red, it would have flushed like a fucking cherry. "You what?!"

He spoke over my outburst. "My manager told me you should keep an eye on it, make sure none of those voices tell you to do anything." He said it with an amused twinkle in his eye, and the tone of his voice was teasing, but I didn't find it funny. Not one bit.

"I'm not crazy!" I blurted louder than I'd planned. "Something's wrong; I'm just sick."

His shoulders rose in a devil-may-care shrug. "Sick has more than one meaning, darlin'."

Appalled, I threw my arms up in frustration and fled the room, furious he would even imply such a thing. Of all the twisted insinuations—I was ready to punch a wall (I nearly did).

Slamming the door shut to my room, I threw myself on the bed and let myself cry. My tears soaked the pillow as I used it to muffle my sobs. I couldn't let Donovan hear. Somehow, I was anxious he'd berate me for crying, and yet I did it anyway. I cried because I ached, I cried because I was sick and not getting better, but most of all, I cried because I was so damn miserable.

* * *

The worst part of my illness was the vomit. Not just because of how gross it was or how much it smelled or how suddenly and violently it came on, but because of the way Donovan treated me when it happened.

We were in the living room. The TV was on, playing some historical drama I was using as a distraction from my pain and never-ending nausea. Donovan was silently reading in his chair. We spoke not a word to each other. Lucy was asleep on the couch cushion next to me, and both the cats were off somewhere taking a hidden nap. Aside from the melodrama on screen, the house was still.

Then it came.

I could feel it stirring. Even though it took less than a second to shoot from my stomach to my mouth, I felt it climb up every inch of my insides and force its way to the surface. The sensation was hot and suffocating, and when I gasped for breath, it erupted. I lurched forward and fell to the floor, landing on my hands and knees. Heaving, I hurled a splash of white foam onto the carpet, followed by another and another. It was as if it never planned to stop.

The foam bubbled and burned in my throat, giving my windpipe little room to let in air. Some of it even built up around my mouth until it eventually drooled from my chin on to the floor. I wanted to expel it all so I could breathe again. Tears squeezed themselves from the corners of my eyes and pooled on my cheeks. My fingers dug into the carpet, uselessly scraping the fibers as if the action would somehow cause the nightmare to end. In my desperation, I looked to Donovan for help. He was on his feet, watching me, a stern expression of fury spread across his face.

It didn't connect with me at first that he was angry. I was so certain a person (especially someone's husband) wouldn't be able to sit by while someone else was in pain. I was sure he'd rush for the phone, medicine, the car keys to take me to the hospital—*something*.

Instead, he yelled at me.

"What the fuck are you doing?" he demanded. "That's *disgusting*. Look what you're doing to the carpet! Do you know how much this cost? Clean that up!"

Even if the vomit hadn't impaired my ability to talk, I would've been speechless. Puking was one thing, but this wasn't normal vomit. Something was wrong. Dangerously wrong—I knew it. He should've been preparing the car to drive me to the emergency room. Instead, he scolded me, reproaching and berating me as if this was entirely my fault. Every word was filled with such malice and conviction, for a moment I was halfway convinced I was to blame for the mess I was making on the living room floor.

But no—*fuck* that, I told myself—that was ridiculous.

Then why was he acting this way?

At last, the eruptions of white foam ceased. I continued to dry heave as though my body wanted to make doubly sure everything had been expelled. Slowly, I got myself under control and was able to breathe properly. Tear runs stained my cheeks, and more were on their way. My throat burned, and the taste in my mouth was vile. Bits of foam still clung to the sides of my mouth. I gasped and sobbed, shaken by the ordeal.

Donovan was still staring at me with discontent. His face was cold and stern. He regarded me with a huff before stepping over me to leave the room.

Over his shoulder, he said, "Get a rag and some cleaner and take care of this."

The room grew still once he left. I remained on the floor for several moments, struggling to find the motivation and strength to stand up. The foam was already soaking into the carpet, crackling as the bubbles popped. I shuddered, repulsed, disgusted, and scared knowing that shit came out of me.

Eventually, I found the resolve to stand. Hands shaking, I wiped off my face with a wet towel and located a fresh rag and some all-purpose cleaner. Kneeling back down to scrub out my vomit, Donovan's words played in my head over and over. The way he spoke, the way he just *watched* as I suffered, made me afraid, angry, and sad all at once.

I dug the rag into the carpet, wanting to scour out both the vomit and the memory. No matter how hard I pressed, none of it went away entirely. I clenched my fist, nails digging into my palm, before I finally shot to my feet and fled to my bedroom, tossing the dirty rag into the laundry room on the way.

For the rest of the night, I remained shut away in my room. The bad taste in my mouth eventually faded away, but I still felt revolting. I cried on and off, trying and failing to push Donovan from my thoughts. I didn't want to see him, not in person and not in my mind's eye. I was pissed, distraught, full of bitterness and heartbreak.

I'd tried. Dammit, I had fucking *tried* to make our marriage work. I'd put up with the pretentiousness, and the weird interests, and the drug dealing, and the snide comments, and the isolation because I foolishly thought things would end happily. I was wrong. Whatever was between me and my husband, it wasn't love. I realized I'd fallen out of love a long time ago but had remained in firm denial. Well, there was no denying it now. I didn't love him. Hell, I'd go so far as to say I hated him. Deeply.

That day was the final nail in the coffin. I knew beyond a reasonable doubt Donovan didn't give a *fuck* about me.

Chapter Eleven

My sickness wavered over the course of eight weeks. In that time, I found myself dropping almost thirty pounds, and I didn't weigh that much to begin with. I was almost resigned to the fact my appetite and sleep schedule would never recover. The auditory hallucinations continued, as did my reddened face. I threw up more white foam on several more occasions.

Thankfully, Donovan wasn't around again to belittle me.

I did make it to the doctor's office more than once. They screened for just about everything they could think of, but couldn't pinpoint the definitive source of my illness. Food allergies were suggested, but changing up my diet didn't do the trick. Something else was going on. Eventually, I became so frustrated with the doctor visits, I stopped them altogether.

Maybe it was stress. After all, I was living with someone who was cooking delicious food for me one minute then verbally abusing me the next. I'd given up on Donovan by that point. I took advantage of his skills as a chef, but beyond that, I was done with him. We didn't love each other, and admitting it was somehow freeing. I no longer felt the need to make things work or please him or garner his attention. Things were over. Emotionally, anyway. On paper, and according to the US government, we were still husband and wife.

That had to change.

A decision Donovan and I seemed to agree upon entirely, as I discovered.

It was the first of August when the van pulled into our driveway. The driver very deliberately backed in close to our garage and stopped just a few feet from the door. At first, I assumed it was a delivery of some kind—maybe something Donovan had ordered for the house. I watched from my bedroom window as Tomas and two other men climbed out and approached the front door.

I groaned. If there was one person on this planet beside Donovan I didn't want to see, it was that shady bastard. Whatever business those two had together, I wanted no part of it. I made sure my door was shut and prepared to read my book and drown them out through the duration of their stay.

The amount of racket they generated made them really difficult to ignore. There was swearing, shifting, heavy footsteps, and the sounds of heavy objects scraping against the floor. It was not helping my headache.

Curiosity got the better of me, and I emerged from my room to see what the hell they were doing. I entered the living room in time to watch Tomas and one of his cronies lift the loveseat and turn it toward the open front door. Donovan was directing them. His eyes flicked toward me and regarded me with a quick, bitter glance.

It didn't deter me. "What the fuck is going on here?" I demanded.

Donovan shrugged. "I'm having the furniture put in storage for a while."

"That's ridiculous—*why?*"

He rolled his eyes and ignored me, returning his attention to the men carrying the loveseat.

Clenching my fists, I stormed back into my room and snatched up my phone. I called my mother and distressingly told her what was happening.

"Call the police," she said without hesitation. "I don't know what he's up to, but call the police."

I held my breath. I knew my mother wasn't Donovan's biggest fan, and I was pissed at him, but... Call the police on my own husband?

That would bring on a whole new layer of separation between us. Despite everything that had happened, I still couldn't let go of the one damn thread of hope and love that connected us together. I'd kept quiet about the cheating and the lying and the drug dealing in favor of keeping the peace. But maybe it was all for nothing. Maybe instead of building a bridge, I had dug a hole.

Maybe there was no peace left to keep.

"Ruby? Are you there?"

Uncertainty hung by a thread. The sounds of furniture bumping the wall in the other room snapped it clean in half.

"Okay," I breathed. "I'll let you know what happens."

"I'll be waiting by the phone. I love you, dear. Be careful."

"I will. Love you."

It took mere minutes for the police to arrive. I stood in the hallway, continuing to observe the men as they proceeded to take away my belongings. Donovan's gaze followed my own to the driveway, where the officer was getting out of his car. Donovan frowned, and I wished I could combat the expression with a triumphant smile, but I was nervous. Something in the air told me anything could happen.

Before entering the house, the officer approached Tomas, regarding him with a nod. He motioned to the van, and Tomas said something I couldn't hear. Then the officer walked up to our front door and knocked.

I tried to answer it, but Donovan got there first.

"Afternoon, officer," he said, slipping into that same charismatic manner he'd displayed long ago when I fell for him. "Something wrong?"

"We had a 911 call from this location."

"It was me," I blurted. I stepped forward to make myself seen. Glancing nervously at Donovan, I continued. "Th-they just showed up and started loading up the furniture. I don't know why, but it needs to stop."

Donovan chuckled and spoke before the officer could respond. "My wife's a little out of the loop. We're just putting things in storage for a hot minute. Sir, if you wait out there for a second, I've got some papers I can show you."

I didn't know anything about these papers, and I was only further confused when the officer agreed and stepped outside to wait in the driveway. Snatching a folder from his desk, Donovan jogged casually back outside and showed them to the officer. Their conversation seemed cordial. Friendly, even.

I watched from the window, unable to hear what was said. It might have been best if I joined them and pushed the matter of how fucked-up the whole situation was, but anxiety rooted me in place. I was afraid to go out and explain myself further in front of Donovan and Tomas. But the officer would come back inside, I reasoned. I was the one who called him in. He'd want to talk to me without the others around. He'd definitely come back in.

He didn't.

Alarm shook me as Donovan and the officer laughed and shook hands. The two made another quick exchange before saying goodbye and the officer returned to his car. My mouth hung open, appalled at what I was seeing. I didn't know much about standard police procedure, but speaking to the person who actually called 911 *alone* seemed like a basic move!

Nothing changed. While Tomas and his friends took no more of the furniture, they shut up what was already loaded in the van and pulled out of the driveway. Which left me and Donovan alone.

He walked slowly through the front door, and I had a million questions for him—like what the fuck was that paperwork for? Why had Tomas come here? Where the hell was our furniture going?

Before I could get a word out, he rounded on me. Reaching out with intense speed, he gripped my arms, and my back hit the wall. I yelped and tried to wrench myself away, but his hold on me was firm. Fingers dug painfully into my flesh. I wanted nothing more than to beg him to let go, but the words were lodged tight in my throat.

"You shouldn't have done that," he growled. "You should have just kept quiet and stayed in your room."

His face. His face was contorted into a horrifying expression that froze me in place. Brows met in a V at the bridge of his nose, and those eyes—those piercing eyes I once found alluring—were black slits hovering above an enraged sneer. It was a stranger's face, a stranger I'd lived with for over a decade. Any memory of love was rapidly being replaced by the sight of that ghastly visage. In that moment, it wasn't human. It was… evil.

My mind begged me to kick and scream. The fear in me was too strong. I was rooted to the spot. Survival instinct pushed me back against the wall, and I willed it to suck me in so I could get away from him.

He peered at me for a while, as if to allow his actions to sink in. Then that awful face softened into something colder and more familiar. He spoke, the smoothness returning to his voice. "I'm still going through with my plan."

Pure confusion sobered me out of silence. "Your plan?"

"And if you figure it out, no one will ever believe you."

My eyes must have been the size of saucers. I could feel them stretching as if the skin around them was even trying to flee. Questions I had, but answers could come later. I just wanted to get away, to get far, *far* away from this monster I'd married.

Donovan, seemingly hellbent on making it all worse, leaned in close. Something held me in place and *did not* let me flinch. Fear? Stubbornness? I like to think it was the latter. I like to think I stood firm out of spite as to not show how intimidated and terrified I was.

All resolve fell away at the sound of his next words:

"If you're not careful, you'll end up like Cindy Song."

Chapter Twelve

I had to get out.

Donovan had already appointed a lawyer. He'd already kicked off the divorce proceedings long before the incident with the furniture. If things had gone his way, he would've divorced me in secret. I rarely saw him around the house since he was too busy going out and doing I-don't-give-a-fuck what. We'd be separated, finally, but it would take time, and divorce was messy, and we were still under one roof and breathing the same air and eating the same food.

And I had to get out.

I called my own lawyer, Gerald. He was an older man and half retired but still practiced law for select clients. I was one of them. Well, my *family* was one of them.

When I recounted the episode about Donovan's friends hauling the furniture away, I could almost hear Gerald shake his head over the phone.

"He can't do that," he told me. "Neither of you can take anything until something's agreed on. He needs to bring it back."

It was almost a triumph to learn Donovan had fucked up. Still, I shuttered at the thought of confronting him about it. "What do I do about it then?"

"Sit tight. I'll handle things from here. Give me a couple days, and I'll touch base."

I didn't tell him about Donovan grabbing me. I didn't tell anyone, actually. Not my friends or siblings or even my parents. I even wore long sleeves to cover the bruises his fingers had left behind. The whole ordeal had frightened me into secrecy. Maybe I should've said something, let someone know what was really going on, but the thought of Donovan discovering my actions unnerved me out of reasonable thought.

No matter how hard I tried, I could not get his threat out of my head.

If you're not careful, you'll end up like Cindy Song.

I'd nearly forgotten about that poor girl. Her disappearance was years ago. That night at the Roadhouse, Tomas had been so boastful about his assurance that he knew what happened to her. You'd think if he'd been lying or kidding, the joke would have died out. For Donovan to bring it up now...

God, I didn't want to think about it.

Then there was the mysterious plan he'd alluded to. What the hell could he possibly be planning? Something with Tomas? The drug rings? Me?

And if you ever figure it out, no one will ever believe you.

I thought back to that time in the Roadhouse, how much distain the hostess and the rest of the staff showed me. Donovan had said something to them, some lie about me to get them to turn on me like that. Greenville was a small town. Everybody knew everyone and everything. People talked, people gossiped. Opinions are formed, and opinions were hard to sway.

Everyone knew Tomas. Tomas had power in Greenville. He and Donovan were good friends. And the way Donovan and the officer acted so chummy...

He told everyone at the restaurant about the voices I'd been hearing. He made me out to be a commanding shut-in. He made everyone hate me.

Oh my god.

He was making everyone think I'm crazy.

No one will ever believe you.

What the fuck had I gotten myself into?

* * *

The furniture did (eventually) come back.

Gerald must have contacted Donovan's lawyer and threatened some nasty legal action. The house became fully furnished once again, though it didn't stay that way for long. Donovan and I had already started divvying up our belongings, but in truth, there wasn't much I wanted. Most of the objects that filled our house were left over from when Julia's parents lived here. It never did feel like it was truly my stuff or my space.

Still, I was happy when Donovan opted to move out.

The vehicle in the driveway was packed to the brim with everything he planned to take. I sat in one of the armchairs that had recently been returned, watching Donovan's every move out of the corner of my eye. I worried if I wasn't discrete about my spying, I'd end up back against the wall again. Or worse.

He couldn't leave fast enough for my comfort. I hoped he would just silently walk out the door and ignore me the way he'd done for years and years, but of course, he didn't. That wasn't his way. He just had to get one final gloat in.

Standing before me, he practically loomed with that same cold, menacing aura he gave off before. He didn't grab me this time, thank God.

"This is still my house," he stated. "I can still come and go as I please, and my friends can come in whenever they like. You'll be seeing me."

I said nothing. Part of me wanted to. Part of me wanted to tell him where he and his friends could stick it. I was pissed, furious at the hell he'd put me through, and there was nothing that would please me more than to stab him with every nasty insult in my vocabulary. Lashing out could prove disastrous, though. I knew what he was capable of and what he wouldn't hesitate to do. I opted to stay quiet and let him have the last word.

The relief I experienced as he left came in waves. The first was when he opened the front door, the next was when he closed it behind him. I got another wave and then another as he climbed into his car and pulled out of the driveway. When he was out of sight, I finally let thirteen years of tension release from my muscles, and I fell back against the chair.

It was done. It was over.

Well… No, it wasn't. Not exactly. The divorce wasn't final. It wouldn't be for a long time. Legal proceedings were a bitch.

He said this was still his house.

I launched from my seat and flew around the house, locking every door and window, pushing away the fact Donovan had a key. The locks would keep the rest of the rabble out, at least.

Once I was done with my task, I let myself breathe. Then I decided to wander the house and see if there was anything of Donovan's he left behind. The last thing I needed was for some secret drug stash to be discovered by a third party.

His room was bare, down to the bedframe. The imprint of his dresser was pressed into the carpet. The closet was empty. I checked every inch to be sure. When I was satisfied, I moved to his bathroom. It too had been stripped of every possible object. The rug and shower curtain had been removed. Even the cleaning supplies under the sink were gone.

There was one thing, though. In a drawer sat a single garden glove, the same one belonging to the pair I'd see him wear while working in the vegetable garden. If this were any other person's bathroom, I would have assumed they simply forgot about it, but this was Donovan. The man was meticulous. Everything to him was symbolic—every gesture, word, and action. He'd been so methodical about removing every single thing from his rooms… except for this glove.

So where was its partner?

There was still a lot I didn't understand about Donovan, but when you've been with someone for so long, it's impossible not to pick up on their quirks, the way they think and behave, how they reason things out. Maybe that's why I headed for my bedroom, why something in my gut told me I would find the second glove there. I checked my bed, my closet, and finally my dresser, where I discovered my assumptions were correct.

The glove was tucked away, crusty and caked with dirt, in the back of my underwear drawer.

That dramatic motherfucker was trying to send me a message.

I needed a drink.

Theories and questions about the gloves wanted to flood my mind, but I shoved them out. Thinking about it felt like giving Donovan the satisfaction of success. He wanted this to rile me, to put me on edge. It was meant to be some reminder of his influence in my life or something. I just knew it.

Dammit, if the gloves didn't do the trick, what I discovered in the kitchen did.

I didn't recognize what it was at first. The thing was sitting in the middle of an otherwise spotless countertop. My first thought was it was a large bug, but as I stepped closer, I found it didn't have legs or antennae. It wasn't living at all, actually. And when I realized what I was looking at, a sickening apprehension churned my stomach more than my constant sickness ever did.

It was a bud.

A single, brown bud from Donovan's mystery plant.

Chapter Thirteen

After disposing of the gloves and that disgusting bud, I was gifted a couple days of peace. Since Donovan's removal from the house, my living space felt freer than before. There's a difference between living alone and living with a person who makes you feel alone. The former is freedom.

I felt well enough to take Lucy for a walk on her leash, something I hadn't been comfortable doing in a long while. The small nagging voice of paranoia prevented me from enjoying my time outside completely, but at least I was *getting* that time. Even though my nausea and headaches continued, resting in my house was easier to do than before. There was no one there to call me lazy, or deny me aid, or laugh at my pain and tell me I was being dramatic.

I could just exist without guilt.

My time was mostly spent relaxing or speaking with Gerald or my parents about the divorce. On more than one occasion, I asked Gerald if there was any way we could speed things along, but of course there wasn't.

"I know you're anxious, but these things take time," he explained to me calmly. There was empathy there, something I hadn't experienced in a while.

I tried to be patient with him, but he was right. I was anxious. Anxious to get out from under Donovan's thumb and never have to think about him or his plan or Tomas or the garden or that goddamn plant ever again.

It would come soon enough, I told myself. I'd just have to be patient.

Patience couldn't stand up to paranoia.

It was during an afternoon in the same week Donovan left when it happened. I noticed something outside my window—a stray dog, I thought. Or a deer, if deer made it that far into the suburbs.

No, neither. It was a person.

A man was in my backyard, looking around as if surveying the place. It was difficult to place him as his head was obstructed by a hood. He had no uniform on to show he belonged to any maintenance company. He was just a guy, trespassing. One of Donovan's friends, most likely, or a member of Tomas' gang of cronies. Honestly, the two groups were probably intersected by that point.

Then I noticed the second man, then the third. There was a whole group of them out there, just walking across my yard. Withholding a scream, I fled from the window and locked myself in my room, drawing the blinds.

I called the police. Donovan wasn't there to charm them away this time. They would have to do their fucking job and hear me out. I waited with bated breath for a knock on the door from an officer. Taking special care not to be seen, I hid out of sight of any windows in case the strangers outside got any ideas. Though they must have known I was home; my car was in the driveway.

They were gone by the time the cops arrived.

Shaking, I gave the officers the best physical description I could of the men, making sure to inform them of my upcoming divorce and my soon-to-be ex-husband's strange behavior.

"Whoever they were, I think they're friends of his," I said, desperately hoping they'd take me seriously. "He might have sent them to torment me or something. I don't know."

God, I must have sounded insane.

The two officers looked at each other, appearing to share some secret exchange between them. One of them fished out a business card from his pocket and handed it to me. It displayed contact information for a Detective Harry Reynolds.

"We'll have Detective Reynolds get in touch with you," he said. "Make sure to tell him exactly what you told us."

"I will," I promised, staring at the card like it was my one-way ticket to peace of mind. "Thank you."

The other officer spoke up. "In the meantime, lock your doors and call us immediately if these men ever come back. Maybe invite a friend over to sit with you."

I nodded, though I couldn't think of anyone I'd want to force into this situation. Maybe my mother could come. I saw no reason why she wouldn't, given my circumstances.

The officers bade me good evening before taking their leave. It unnerved me to watch them go. As their cruiser rolled away, I wished I'd requested a guard of some kind—maybe a single officer to park outside my house and keep an eye on things. But I had the idea too late, and it seemed like a waste of their time to call 911 and ask them to come out again.

But being alone was the last thing I wanted. I called my mother over and resigned to wait until I heard from the detective to do anything further.

It only took a day for him to get in contact. I was invited to the local station for to speak with him and make a formal report. Detective Reynolds was an older man, a little gruff and a little too overworked. And he got right to the point. "I understand you've had some trespassers on your property."

"Yes," I said, glancing to the window, half expecting the men to be standing outside, spying on me. "There must have been four or five of them just walking around. It looked like they were surveying the yard or something."

"Did you recognize any of them?"

"Not really." I wished I had. If I could have offered up even one name, I could foresee real legal action taking place. As it stood, I had next to nothing. "I hid in my house as soon as I saw how many there were."

"I see. That was probably for the best, for the sake of your safety." He paused, making a quick note and lifting the piece of paper to check the one underneath. "And this is the second time you've contacted us in recent days."

The statement sounded like an invitation, so I launched right into it. "Yes, I called before because my husband Donovan and his friends were loading up all our furniture. He didn't tell me why or what he was doing with it, but I found out later he was getting ready to divorce me. My lawyer told me he couldn't just take everything like that."

"Right, right. Where are your belongings now?"

"Back in the house."

"Alright, good." He scratched something down with his pen.

I bit my lip, knowing full well I couldn't leave things at that. Who knew when I'd have a detective's full attention again? "Th-there's something else," I began nervously.

The detective was all business but not unkind. He looked up and replied, "Yes, go on," shortly but encouragingly.

Clutching the sides of my seat, the words caught in my mouth. My legs shook with apprehension. Fighting my nerves, I stammered out, "When the officer and everyone left, um…"

There was a pause. The detective was looking at me, his attention severed completely from his paperwork.

"What happened when everyone left?"

I swallowed. "Donovan came back inside and he… Well, he grabbed me. Um… H-he threatened me—something about his plan—he said I'd end up like Cindy Song if I wasn't careful." The latter half of it came out like a ramble, and my heart rate accelerated to the point where I worried my heart would leap right out of my chest. "You know about Cindy Song, right?"

"I do, yes." As panicked as I was, Detective Reynolds kept calm. "Did he tell you anything else?"

"He said this was still his house, that he and his friends could come back whenever they wanted."

"So, you think these trespassers are a sign of him following up on that statement?"

"Yes, exactly."

I was still shaking, both out of nerves and a strange excitement that things were happening. Detective Reynolds' gaze trailed down to the bruises on my legs.

"Is that where he grabbed you?" he asked, brow furrowed.

"No. I don't know how I got these. I've been sick lately—they just appeared."

He nodded, and I could tell he was contemplating my statements. "All the same, I'd like to take pictures for our records."

"Yeah." I spoke in a near sigh. "Do whatever you need to do."

The detective asked me a few more questions about Donovan and our time together. I answered everything as best I could, and after an hour passed, he took pictures of my legs and told me he planned to speak with Donovan before getting back in touch with me. The thought made me queasy.

"In the meantime, we'll see what we can do about these men on your lawn." He stood, ready to escort me out of his office. "No guarantees, but we'll sure as hell try."

I thanked him, but without any names or any distinctive features I could provide, I knew their search for these would-be intruders would come up with nil. They wouldn't find them. Those men could come back.

Donovan could come back.

The moment I got home from the station, I snatched up the phone to call a locksmith. No one was getting in. The locks *had* to be changed.

Getting those fucking things installed was the best idea, as it turned out. True to his word, Detective Reynolds had spoken with Donovan, which resulted in me receiving an angry phone call.

"The hell are you doing talking with the police?" Donovan demanded. "Did you not understand what I said to you?"

I tried to let anger override my nerves. "Well, what the fuck do you expect me to do?"

"Sit tight and shut up. I've got enough on my plate, I don't need all this extra shit."

"*You've* got enough on your plate? I'm—" I clenched my jaw and pounded my fist on the arm of my couch. "Don't talk to me anymore. We're done."

"We're not done by a long shot. And if you don't want to hear from me, then don't give me a reason to call again."

He hung up before I could tell him to fuck off.

Detective Reynolds suggested I get a restraining order, but I firmly shot down the idea. I worried taking further action was just going to piss off Donovan all the more, and I couldn't imagine him respecting the order anyway. He'd come after me for sure if he found out, and he wasn't that far away to begin with. I discovered through the grapevine of Greenville's gossip that Donovan had moved into an apartment only two miles down the street. He was so close. I knew he'd gone out of his way to find the nearest possible place so he could keep an eye on me.

So yes, the locks were changed, and they would remain changed, a decision Gerald gave me hell about.

"It's still his house, Ruby. Both your names are on the deed until we get your matters finalized." He sounded nearly exasperated but still kind. "Legally, he can't be locked out of it. I'm sorry, but you need to put the old locks back on."

"No, I can't," I insisted. "I don't feel…" *safe.* "I don't feel comfortable about it."

"Is there anywhere you can go that *would* make you feel comfortable?"

Actually, there was.

The next morning, I took a drive to my parents' house to spend the day with my mother. The change of scenery would do me some good, I decided, and I just needed someone to talk to in person that wasn't a lawyer or a cop.

As we settled in the living room with a pitcher of water between us, she commented on my weight. I hadn't even come close to regaining those lost thirty pounds, and I was beginning to look gaunt. My head felt hazy, and the nausea continued to persist, but I made no mention of any of it.

Mom grilled me on my diet, my sleep schedule, all those things mothers are supposed to worry about. I gave her my answers as truthfully as I could without outright lying. My health was in poor condition, but I didn't want her to fret about me more than she already did. Besides, I feared that if I dove into all my symptoms, things would spiral into me spouting speculations about mystery plants and drug rings and some plot of Donovan's to make people think I was crazy, and what mother wants to hear that from her child? Just the thought of it made me almost wonder if I *was* crazy. Instead, I did my best to try to make this as normal a visit as possible.

"I'm glad that son of a bitch is out of your house," she said, swerving from the discussion of my daily habits. "I don't want to say I told you so, Ruby, but you know I never liked him."

"I know, I'm sorry." I practically hung my head because, honestly, I *was* sorry. Sorry I didn't listen to the people around me before it was too late and I'd lost over a decade to my biggest mistake.

Mom patted my hand. "Don't apologize. It's going to be over soon. We just need those divorce papers finalized and then you can move on with your life."

"That's what I'm hoping."

As I moved to take a drink of my water, she let out a gasp that nearly made me drop the glass.

"Sweetie, what did you do to your legs?" she asked, already leaving forward to inspect them.

"My legs?" I lifted one up to see what she meant.

The bruises. I'd nearly forgotten.

"What did you do?" Mom asked again.

"I have no idea," I admitted truthfully.

"You didn't fall or anything?"

"I don't think so."

She looked at me with a suddenly fierce expression; probably the same one lions give their prey before they pounce. "Did he—"

"No. He didn't." I tried to forget about the still-fading bruises on my arms underneath my cardigan. "Mom, I *really* don't know how I got these."

"Well, we need to go to the hospital, right now. Come on, get your purse. I'll drive."

We hurriedly piled into her car, and as we drove down the road, I was struck by the memory of when Donovan denied me that trip to the emergency room after I'd vomited up all that foam. The swiftness with which my mother had acted made me want to cry.

I held it in.

* * *

It wasn't a long wait to get into the emergency room. All my movements were a blur as I stripped down, gowned up, and was settled into an uncomfortable bed. Mom sat by my side. She held my hand while the nurse took stock of my vitals, claiming they were all normal.

A phone buzzed, and Mom checked her messages. Her shoulders lowered with a sliver of a relieved sigh.

"Your father's on his way," she told me.

"Oh, good." It would be nice to have them both there. Though I couldn't help but feel guilty that I'd given them cause to worry.

Dad arrived before the doctor did. He stood at the doorway, stopping in his tracks at the sight of me. There was concern on his face, sure, but I saw contemplation in his expression, like the gears were turning, trying to reason something out. Outside of a quick greeting and a kiss on my cheek, he said nothing as Mom brought him up to speed.

When the doctor came, he wasted no time before checking my legs. He asked me all the typical questions: When did I notice these? Has this happened before? Did I have any recent falls? The inquiries grew more specific as he tried to weed out the common ailments. I answered to the best of my ability, though at times I found it hard to form a complete thought. My head was so cloudy, I didn't think to bring up any of my other symptoms.

The silent seconds between each question grew longer as the doctor grappled with what to ask me next. He wanted to know if I was taking any blood thinners. When I told him no, he seemed stumped.

After reconvening with some colleagues outside the room, the doctor came back in and said, "We're going to perform an ultrasound and do some blood work to see if we can determine what's causing this."

"Is there anything you can give her to get rid of them?" Mom asked.

The doctor squared his shoulders. "Possibly, but I don't want to prescribe anything until we know what we're dealing with."

I held my breath throughout the ultrasound, hoping it would shed light on what was happening. Only disappointment met me when it came up with nothing. It'd be another day before the test results came back from the blood work. Since there was no immediate reason to keep me in the hospital, the doctor told me I could go home but with instructions to take it easy and let him know if anything new cropped up.

On they way back to my parents' house, I leaned my head against the window in thought. Like everything else, I hadn't mentioned the men who had trespassed on my lawn. A sickening anxiety settled in, telling me they would return. I almost convinced myself they were already there, hidden in the house and waiting. For all I knew, it could be Donovan, Tomas, and their crew. The thought nearly shortened my breath. I couldn't take it. I couldn't be alone.

"Mom?" It came out more panicked than I'd prefer.

"Hm?" She glanced at me, not taking her eyes off the road for more than a second.

"Is it alright if I stay with you and Dad for a while?"

There was no hesitation. "Of course you can! I had half a mind to ask myself."

"Can we swing by my house now?" I asked, failing to hide my urgency. "I just want to get my stuff and go."

She raised an eyebrow, clearly suspecting something was up. "Ruby, is there something you're not telling me?"

"Donovan still has keys to the house, and I can't lock him out, and—" I cut myself off to take a breath. My hands shook and wrung together anxiously. The next thing I said was practically frantic. "C-can we just go? Please?"

Mom blinked, taken aback by my tone, but she turned down a road to my house and picked up her phone. "Yeah, we'll swing by. Let me call your father…"

As she talked things over with Dad (he agreed right away I should stay with them), I let myself fall back into my seat and try to breathe at a normal rate. I was sitting on the precipice of this whole nightmare being over, and it wasn't coming fast enough. Maybe separating myself physically from the situation really was the best option.

My parents helped me pack. I didn't take much, just some clothes, toiletries, and everything the animals would need. Loading it all into the car had a sense of finality to it. I knew what still sat inside the house— the kitchenware, appliances, and all that furniture I'd fought so hard to get back. I wanted none of it now. Every piece of it reminded me of what I'd lived with, what I'd gone through, and what could still lie around the bend. To hell with it. The only thing that mattered to me now was to escape. I was going to leave that house.

And I was never going back.

Chapter Fourteen

I was out.

Finally, *finally*, I was out.

I should have been more celebratory about the fact, but it was impossible to be so cheery, given the legal matters still tying Donovan and me together. The divorce wasn't final, and it wouldn't be for months. Gerald warned me it could be a long road ahead still, which made me want to dig a deep hole and bury myself in it. My parents, bless them, told me I could stay with them as long as I needed.

It would be a while.

As if the stress of divorce and fear for my safety weren't enough, I still felt sick. By that point, I'd almost forgotten what it was like to feel well. Being nauseous and fighting a headache and hearing strange noises became my default state. I longed for it to end.

The blood work came back from the lab. It turned up nothing. The doctor's ideas of what it could be ran dry, and all he could tell me was to take it easy and let them know if the bruises every reappeared. Maybe then they could pinpoint a cause.

There was no way I could hide my suffering from my mother while I was living under her roof. She was always the most observant one in the family, and you just can't keep everything from the woman who raised you. Again, she expressed concern about my lost weight and fretted over me enough to the point where I let her in about my other symptoms.

"How long as this been going on?" she asked.

Her face grew pale when I told her.

We took another trip to the doctor's office. Mom got it in her head there was something wrong with my thyroid, and she wanted them to perform some tests. I had a sliver of hope she was right, and that I could finally figure out what was wrong with me and take steps to treat it, but—*goddammit*—once again, we'd hit a dead end. My thyroid was just fine. It was the rest of me that was fucked.

I was so tired. Every day, I struggled the energy needed to get out of bed failed me. If I wasn't meeting with Gerald or tending to Lucy and the cats, I was practically a vegetable. My days were spent in bed or on the couch, trying to relax and find some semblance of peace with my situation. It became apparent that wasn't going to happen anytime soon, so instead I filled my time with escapism. I watched TV, read books, did *anything* to distract myself from thinking about the last thirteen years of my life.

My efforts didn't always work. Sometimes I'd spot something moving across the window out of the corner of my eye and jolt in fear, only for it to simply be a car driving by. At night, my auditory hallucinations seemed heightened by the silent stillness of the house, and on more than one occasion, I thought someone had broken in and was coming for me. I lost sleep worrying about it. I'd mutter nervous comforts to myself, trying to convince myself I was away from Donovan and I was in a safe place—I would *not* end up like Cindy Song.

It did very little to calm me down.

A week went by, then two, and during the third week, I found myself miraculously getting better. The fog shrouding my mind began to clear, and it felt like a weight hampering my head was lifted. My headaches subsided. The redness of my skin went away. I was clear of bruises. The nausea stopped, and the noises ceased to haunt me. Conversations with my parents, my friends, and Gerald became easier to hold, and aside from my persisting paranoia regarding Donovan, I was close to feeling like my old self.

With this newfound clarity, I finally allowed myself to think. The affairs of the divorce and my illness were all I'd tried to concentrate on since I moved in with my parents, but now I contemplated what could have been wrong with me. It was strange. Weeks and weeks of suffering, only for it to just fade away so simply and on its own. What the hell could it have possibly been? Stress? Fear for my life? No, I still had plenty of both.

Something had to have changed. Switching living spaces couldn't heal a person of something so severe, not without any sort of treatment—right? No, I must have been doing something different to make it all go away. But what the fuck was it? I had no new medications, my drinking habits were the same, I wasn't exercising any more than usual, and my diet—

My diet.

Donovan cooked. Donovan *always* cooked for me, despite how much distance he'd put between us in the last seven years. Yet he always made us dinner. That was a constant. I'd assumed it was just because of his passion for cooking. What a stupid way to kid myself. Deep down, I knew that passion didn't come from a love of the culinary arts for art's sake. I should've known. That bastard told me what he was all about the fucking day we met:

If you control what a person eats, then you control them.

The speed at which everything clicked into place was frightening. Starting with that plant—that *fucking* plant! He wouldn't let me know what it was. Of course he didn't. You don't tell prey what bullet you're using before you shoot it. And if I'd had a chance to look it up, I might have suspected something, and he couldn't have that. Christ, he even had Tomas bring it in from Panama—harder to recognize a foreign plant.

My stomach churned. That had been so long ago. He'd planned this. He'd planned this for months. And then he left that bud and those gloves as hints to mock me.

As I sat there, pale faced and shaken by this revelation, my father returned home from work. He came straight to the living room and poked his head in.

"How're you feeling, sweetie?" he asked.

"Better," I said, trying to come across that I was glad for the fact. I was, of course, but given recent developments I wouldn't be surprised if the nausea came back. "A lot better, actually. It's weird. It just went away."

"That's good, though." Dad sounded happy for me, but I could tell he too was hiding some cautious apprehension. "Anything wrong?"

I bit my lip. The idea of saying it out loud seemed to add more credence to it, like if I spoke the words, it would deem it all as truth. As much as I wanted to get to the bottom of my illness, this was the last thing I'd ever want it to be.

But I couldn't keep this to myself.

"Dad, do you think Donovan could have been poisoning me?"

He took a deep breath, and I wondered if he'd call me crazy for even conceiving such an idea. Then he shook his head in a way that told me he agreed. "My God, that's what I thought in the emergency room. I didn't want them to think I was seeing little green men."

We had that in common.

Dad sat himself next to me and sighed. "Maybe I should have said something."

"It's alright," I told him. Honestly, I was just happy someone believed me and was on my side. "I'm better now, so it's over."

"Do you know what he could've been using, though?"

"Yes," I admitted and told him all about the mystery plant, how Tomas had brought the seeds overseas and he and Donovan kept its name secret from me. Dad crossed his arms and leaned back in thought.

"So, you have no idea what it is?"

"No. It's some plant from Panama, or just somewhere in Central America. That's all I got."

"I see." His brow furrowed as he stared sternly ahead. "Well, since we don't know what it is, we don't know everything it's been doing to you. I think you need to make an appointment with Doctor Collins. I've been seeing him for years, I trust his judgment. He might be able to figure something out."

I shook my head, my stomach plummeting at the thought of pursuing it further. "No, I can't take any more of this."

"Ruby, you've been poisoned. We don't know all the effects this thing has." He placed his hand on mine. "I want to make sure you're okay."

"I *am*," I insisted. Frustrated tears bit at the corners of my eyes. "Dad, all of this has been so hard to deal with. I'm terrified, and I need all of this to be over. I just want to hide my head in the sand and move on!"

"Alright, alright, easy now." He wrapped his arm around me and pulled me close. "Just think about it, okay?"

I nodded to please him, but I knew I wouldn't change my mind.

Mom came home not long after. Dad helped me inform her about our poisoning theory. Judging by the look on her face, I'd say if Donovan had been in the room, I would've been doing business with a morgue instead of a divorce attorney.

Again, Dad tried to convince me to see his doctor about all this, and again, I turned him down, continuing with my stance of how much I wished to put it all behind me. Though as a compromise, I offered to call the police and make a report.

"Detective Reynolds has already talked to Donovan," I said. "Maybe he can use this in a case against him. We could get the motherfucker locked up."

"With what proof?" Mom challenged. "It's your word against his, Ruby. I guarantee he's removed all trace of that plant from your garden."

"Do you still have that bud he left behind?" Dad asked.

I shook my head, suddenly disappointed with myself. "No, I didn't even think to keep it. I was so disgusted, I just threw it away."

"Then we have nothing," Mom concluded. "So, I agree, let's keep this all behind us. There's no telling what the son of a bitch might do if he finds out we got the authorities involved again, and I can't risk—" She stopped short, taking a deep breath before pulling me into a tight hug. "No, let's get you through this divorce, then move on."

It was settled, then. We all got on the same page, deciding I should keep a low profile until the divorce was final and then figure out what to do from there—a task that was easier said than done.

Chapter Fifteen

The following months, I remained hidden from the world. I didn't go out, I didn't have visitors, and definitely didn't return to my house. Just as I had done before living under the same roof as Donovan, I lived in isolation. Except this time, instead of being cut off by depression or neglect, this was under the intent of self-preservation. Donovan was still chummy with Tomas, and Tomas's reach in Greenville was too wide. Anyone on the street could be in league with them, and so I took no chances. I didn't want to be seen. I didn't want Donovan to know anything about my movements while we were still bound together by a marriage license.

As one would imagine, I had a lot of time on my hands. Try as I might to escape my previous predicament, I couldn't stop thinking about it. It sickened me all over again to know I'd been living with someone who was so willing and ready to do much so much harm. The more I thought about it, the more I was certain Donovan had been poisoning me. It was the only conclusion that explained every single one of his actions.

Nothing was a coincidence with this man. Donovan was all about fate and symbolism and all that crap. He could sleep through his morning alarm and find some bullshit deeper meaning in it. If he had planned this plot against me, then he was sure to have figured it out down to the letter.

I revisited the plant, his weapon of choice; he'd asked Tomas to bring those seeds back from Central America specifically to do me in. I shuddered as it dawned on me just how much Donovan had gotten me involved with the growth and care of this thing. The day he made me dig those rocks from the dirt suddenly had a reason to it. He'd wanted me to prepare the earth for planting with my own two hands. Then he recruited me again to take the seedlings outside so they could soak in the sun. He had me out there with him, nearly every day, working and weeding that garden plot, mere feet from the very cause of my illness.

It was so cruelly ritualistic, the way he'd forced my participation. Almost like it was necessary for my hands to be involved in the process. I felt sick all over again wondering if this was some Satanist rite or ritual.

That's why he didn't stake the tomatoes. It was never about the vegetables. It was all a front just to grow that one damned plant—that *thing* he'd planned to torture and possibly kill me with. Our plot was even in the far corner of the community garden. Tomas had secured the spot for us. The placement had been curated so it would see the smallest amount of foot traffic. Less people walking by meant less chances for someone to notice we were growing something unusual.

That wasn't even the full extent of it, I realized. The day we'd taken Lucy to the vet—that awful face he made—that was part of it. Feeding grapes to our dog, giving her a UTI on purpose, it was a preview of things to come. A demonstration of his power. He had shown me firsthand the extent of what he was capable of. I kicked myself for not seeing it sooner.

As I sat and parsed out recent events, a cascade of thoughts and understandings sent my mind racing. He'd used me to acquire drugs to sell. He'd taken advantage of my parents' money to better his lifestyle. And the moment we were married, the moment we were locked into a relationship and a mortgage and I was under his thumb, that's when he flipped the switch. No more nights of escape, no more romantic sweet nothings. He'd courted me just to get me alone and tied to him.

Somehow, that was a worse pill to swallow than poisoning my food.

One thing I couldn't pinpoint was *why*. Why go through all this trouble of marrying me, living with me for so long, only to try to do me in like this? Was he really just that much of a sick fuck?

That had to be it. I couldn't wrangle any other possible explanation from the life we had shared together. Donovan thought of himself as this being with great power, and he lorded it all over me simply because he could. I'd married a true-blue Satanist, and that's what I got.

If only I could get rid of him faster.

As I waited impatiently for the legal proceedings to reach their end, something cropped up that shed a little light on Donovan's motives. Gerald had been in frequent contact with Donovan's lawyer, and one day he called me with an interesting bit of news:

"Apparently, Donovan is under the impression there's a seventy-thousand dollar equity on your house."

"What?" I almost laughed. Gerald and I had reviewed my assets enough times for me to know that wasn't true. "Where on earth did he get that idea?"

"It wasn't clear, but he was fighting hard for the house before. He might not be so keen on it when he discovers it's not worth what he thought. If he drops it, things could accelerate to an agreement."

Just the prospect of this nightmare coming to an end brought me relief. "That'd be ideal," I said through a sigh. "I want this to be over like you wouldn't believe."

"I know, Ruby. Divorces are rarely very clean. We're doing all we can to wrap things up, but it's going to take time."

I told him I understood, but there was a nagging churning in my stomach that wanted him to hurry, whatever the cost.

Donovan's assumption about our house's net worth birthed a possible explanation for the timing of his actions. It was clear to me now. I could almost visualize the gears turning in his head as he plotted his scheme.

If the house *did* hold such a high equity, it would all go to him should anything happen to me. But how would he get a hold of it? Divorce couldn't have been an appealing option at the time, given the value of the house would either be split or assigned to only one of us. He didn't want to risk me getting a dime, so he resorted to a more profitable option: disposing of me.

He couldn't simply have me killed, no. That'd be too easy to trace back to him. I don't even think Tomas's influence could scrub him of a murder charge. Besides, a quick death on my part wasn't Donovan's style. He was sick, demented—he wanted that slow burn, that demonstration of his power to validate his culinary profession and render me helpless.

Poisoning it was, then.

From there, it was a matter of getting the seeds from Tomas and growing the cause of my misery right under my nose. It must have made him so giddy to get me involved, to watch me nurture the plant he'd assigned to my cause of death. Meanwhile, he spread rumors about me to make everyone in town believe I was crazy. It was social insurance. If I ever figured out what was happening, anyone I told would think I was insane or lying, and Donovan would maintain his favorable, sympathetic stance in the community.

There was just one problem, though: I wouldn't die. I'd grown sick and weak and relied on him more than ever, but I just wouldn't die. I thought of how he mocked me the first day my symptoms arose; he was certainly celebrating his upcoming triumph over my life. How frustrating it must have been for him to realize the poison was doing its work without finishing the job. Hell, that time he berated me for vomiting white foam could've been an expression of his own frustration that I was still alive.

Maybe it became clear to him he couldn't kill me through food, not in the way he planned. Maybe he grew frustrated and impatient, and so he went with plan B and contacted a divorce lawyer. And the rest, I understood.

Yes, that felt right. The amount of sense it made to me was frightening, and I was furious with myself for not seeing through Donovan sooner. It took a near-death experience to shake me from my stupor, and now that I was awake, I was ashamed and terrified. You hear about people like Donovan, about people who are so twisted and evil, they get it in their head they can destroy another person's life with malice and cunning. The idea was sensational, something one would read in a novel or see on TV. You never expect to meet such a person in real life. Now that I had, it made me want to hide from the whole rotten, dangerous world for as long as I could.

It was a comfort to know he failed in his endgame, but the fact he played at all would haunt me forever.

* * *

The final divorce papers came in on Valentine's Day, but it felt more like Christmas. I cried when I opened the envelope. Hands shaking with relief, I read the fine print again and again. It was official. Donovan and I were separated physically *and* in the eyes of the law. The nightmare, at last, was over.

Where did I go from here?

The question surprised me. I'd been so focused on ridding myself of this marriage, I hadn't put any thought into what I would do after. The house was mine, as the settlement decreed, but I suddenly had no desire to go back. There were too many memories there, too many reminders. The place could burn to the ground for all I cared.

"Don't worry about it," my mother told me when I expressed my concerns. She beamed at the documentation severing me from that monster. "It's all over now. Just relax and take some time to recover."

"You can stay with us as long as you need," my father added.

I was grateful to them both. They were offering a sanctuary, and I fell into it with open arms. For weeks, I remained under their roof. I should have felt safe and secure, but I couldn't shake the paranoia that Donovan wasn't through with me. There were anxious moments where I would glance at my phone and worry that missed call notification was from him. Cars passing by continued to make me tense up with fear. I worried it was Donovan checking in on me—or worse, *coming* for me.

After a time, when nothing horrible happened, I felt confident enough to venture out of the house on a more regular basis. I tried to establish a routine, which included a daily walk with Lucy around the block. The fresh air did me a mountain of good, and the exercise helped clear my head. It was peaceful in my parents' neighborhood, and I soon experienced a sense of protection within the vicinity.

I wished I hadn't grow so comfortable.

Around mid-March, Detective Reynolds contacted me, requesting I come into his office and answer a few questions he had regarding Cindy Song. He sounded insistent, but I had to insist right back that I couldn't do it.

"Greenville's a small town. News travels fast," I told him. "I know if I go, Donovan will find out. Besides, if I'm being honest, there isn't much to tell."

"I understand, Ruby, but Cindy's family has mourned the loss of their daughter for years now. Any information you have might help them find some long overdue closure."

"I… I don't know…" It was a horrible idea, given how furious Donovan had been the last time I'd visited the detective. Things were supposed to be over between us. Any movement on my part could put him back on my trail, and the thought terrified me.

Detective Reynolds spoke through my thoughts. "Ruby, what if it was your child missing?"

I closed my eyes, thinking about the worry and hurt on my mother's face when I told her of Donovan's abuse against me. That poor girl's mother must have felt so much worse knowing she'd never see her daughter again…

I agreed to meet with him.

The drive to the station was nerve-wracking. I kept looking over my shoulder, paranoid I'd be spotted by the wrong set of eyes. Parking my car in the most discrete spot in the lot, I triple checked my surroundings before I rushed into the building. Detective Reynolds didn't keep me waiting, knowing full well I wanted this meeting to be as short as possible. We wasted little time on pleasantries and dove straight into the questioning.

For all my trouble, I wished I had more to tell the detective. Outside of Tomas boasting that he knew Cindy's fate and location, and Donovan's threat against me, there wasn't much else to offer. If Detective Reynolds was expecting me to be a fountain of clues he could use to blow this cold case wide open, he'd be disappointed.

"I'm *certain* the two of them know what happened to her," I stated with conviction. "Tomas is so shady, and he was way too proud and eager to talk about Cindy. And Donovan… He's a twisted monster, he'd love to be part of something like this."

The conversation was riling me, but the detective remained calm. "Do you suspect they're the cause of Cindy's disappearance?"

Admittedly, I wasn't sure on that front. "Maybe. At least Tomas. As far as I know, he and Donovan met after Cindy disappeared. But they're close. If Tomas did kidnap and—" Saying the word "kill" suddenly felt too close to home. "If he took Cindy and wanted to tell someone about it, it would probably be Donovan."

It became apparent to Detective Reynolds I didn't have much in the way of proof, so he switched to questioning me about Tomas and Donovan's character, especially the former. I had nothing nice to say, of course. However, I made no mention of the drug rings, afraid if I gave away too much information, I'd become a target. It was possible Detective Reynolds was already aware of them anyway. Even if he wasn't, it wouldn't take much investigating on his part to discover Tomas's criminal activity. I was here for Cindy, nothing more.

The detective exhausted everything out of me I was willing to give him and then we said our goodbyes. I made it home without incident, and after a few days of hiding away in my parents' house, I convinced myself it was safe to venture back outside.

About a week after my meeting with Detective Reynolds, I decided to go for a walk. My parents were gone on vacation, so it was just me and Lucy doing our usual route down the block. On our way back, I noticed a van parked outside the house. At first, I assumed it was some repair man or a plumber, but the vehicle had no markings. It was just a white van parked directly in front of my parents' house, still running.

Then I noticed the driver was staring at me.

Panic seized me. I didn't bother leading Lucy to the house—instead, I scooped her up and rushed to the front door as quickly as I could. Somehow, I still had the presence of mind to check the van's license plate. Bursting into the house, I muttered the plate's numbers repeatedly under by breath so I wouldn't forget it. I snatched my phone and locked the door with one motion, not hesitating for a moment to dial 911. As I waited for the operator to pick up, I stared out the window. The van was leaving. Whoever was in there must have been waiting for me.

I gave the police the best description of the van I could, including the license plate number. They asked me questions: Did I recognize the driver? No, the window was too tinted to get a good look. Though I had a feeling.

Once I hung up, I drew all the blinds over the windows and made a beeline to the liquor cabinet. I burst into tears after two vodka shots.

Later, I received a call from the police: the license plate on that van had been reported stolen.

I couldn't stay here.

My parents arrived home two days later, and I was already packed to go. They agreed after this van incident, I wasn't safe in Greenville. We made swift plans for me to move to another state, as far away as I could without needing a plane ticket to visit home. Where would I live? I'd figure that out when I got there.

My phone number was changed, and I deleted any and all social media accounts. Mom asked if I wanted to go back to my house and grab anything from there. I couldn't. It would only add more time to my move, and the possibility Donovan would discover I was leaving was too great a risk to take. Nothing was more important to me than running the hell away.

I told no one of my flight, not even my friends. Greenville was as toxic to my wellbeing as that mysterious plant, and I could only trust my parents with my movements and location. It hurt to go, to step away so suddenly from everything I'd ever known, but it was the only way. I had to free myself from all the fear and conspiracy. I had to hide and protect myself from the demon I'd tolerated for so long.

I had to survive.

With everything in place, we packed up my car—all the clothes I had, plus my pets and their belongings—and I was ready to go. Dad accompanied me on the drive. He wanted to make sure whatever place I ended up in was clean and safe. We drove for hours, crossing several state lines until we reached the destination of my choosing. Luckily, it didn't take long for us to put me up in a single bedroom apartment. There was no furniture, and I had nothing to fill the place with. I bought some foldout chairs and a mattress to sleep on; I'd worry about the rest of the furnishings later.

Dad flew back to Greenville after I was settled. Once again, I was alone, and for the first time in my life I was more than glad for it. *Alone* meant no one would take advantage of me or threaten my life. I was hidden away and secure, living day-to-day burdened by the hell I'd gone through—the mistakes I'd made. Through the quiet days and lonely nights, I tried to cope, grappling reconciliation with one hand and nursing a bottle with the other. Nightmares plagued me, and tears made frequent visits. Nothing brought me the peace I so jealously sought.

And I'm still searching for it.

Conclusion

It's been over eight years since I fled the state.

I spent that time living in fear and isolation, trying to recover from everything I've been through. One would think after so much time passed, I'd be comfortable living a normal life again, but paranoia still grips me. The nightmares, the trauma, the fear for my safety—they may never go away.

Aside from close family and friends, very few people know where I am. I'm about as off the grid as you can be in the modern era. I keep all online activity private; I have no public social media presence. Still, every now and then I check in on Donovan through the web. He was never arrested or convicted of any of his crimes. With no hard proof to promote legal action, I was unable to make a solid case against my ex-husband. I would never have my day in court. I would never look a judge in the eye, point at my attempted murderer, and say, "He poisoned me, your honor. For over two months, he poisoned my food and tried to kill me."

For years, I tried to figure out what that plant was. I've consulted dozens of books and online resources, but I couldn't find anything that came close to what grew in our garden plot. If this were a work of fiction, I'm sure I would've uncovered the species name or stumbled upon it accidentally in some greenhouse and recognized it by sight. But this isn't fiction, and I still have no idea what to call that *thing* Donovan put in my food. The poisonous plant from Panama will forever remain a mystery.

I never heard from Detective Reynolds again. Whatever efforts he might have made toward putting Donovan and Tomas behind bars were all for naught. They're still out there, living perfectly happy lives. Donovan married, the same woman from the Roadhouse he cheated on me with. They have two children, and all four of them smile in every picture I see; online at least, Donovon appears to be the perfect family man. I have no knowledge of said family's mental health or wellbeing.

As time passed, my horrid experience seemed to grow distant from the rest of the world. Looking back, I wonder what would have happened if I'd gone to the police or the press with my story—the *full* story. Would Donovan be in jail now? Would Tomas's drug rings have crumbled?

Would Cindy Song's abductor and murderer have been caught?

There's still no doubt in my mind those two know what happened to that girl. No one can convince me otherwise. After all, Donovan told me if I wasn't careful I'd end up like her, and that's a memory I'll never be able to wipe away.

In a way, the monster was right: Cindy's perpetrators were never caught, and neither were mine. Except, everyone knew Cindy's story, and she's dead; I'm alive, but no one knows the hell I endured. I got away. I won, but I'm wounded—survival at a price. Here I am in my forties, practically afraid of my own shadow, suffering in silence. All the while, the man who tried to do me in still walks free.

That's why people have to know.

Someone *has* to know. Even if justice never comes through for me, I can concoct my own closure. After years of therapy, meditation, and contemplation, I finally felt I was in a position to revisit my life's tragedy and share it with the world. That doesn't mean it was easy, but it was doable.

Now you know. And I hope if anyone reading this finds themself in a position where a loved one puts their safety and life at risk, they take action. Speak out. Make your suffering known. Don't be afraid to

separate yourself from the one who abuses you.
Let yourself escape…
Before it's too late.

Anna Miller

According to the National Coalition Against Domestic Abuse, more than ten million people in the United States experience domestic abuse each year. If you or someone you know feels unsafe at home, please contact the following number:

National Domestic Violence Hotline
1-800-799-7233

Anna Miller

Copyright © 2021 by Anna Miller All rights reserved

www.ingramcontent.com/pod-product-compliance
Lightning Source LLC
Chambersburg PA
CBHW022341280326
41934CB00006B/730

* 9 7 8 0 5 7 8 3 0 2 5 6 0 *